CLASSIC SERMONS ON THE CHURCH

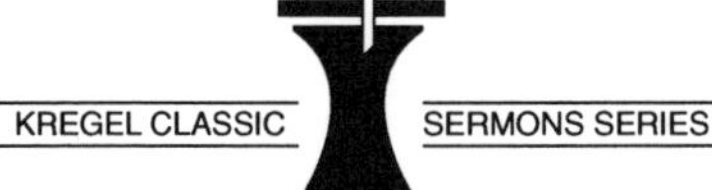

CLASSIC SERMONS ON THE CHURCH

Compiled by

Warren W. Wiersbe

Grand Rapids, MI 49501

Classic Sermons on the Church
Compiled by Warren W. Wiersbe

Published by Kregel Publications, a division of Kregel, Inc., P.O. Box 2607, Grand Rapids, MI 49501. Kregel Publications provides trusted, biblical publications for Christian growth and service. Your comments and suggestions are valued.

For more information about Kregel Publications, visit our web site at http://www.kregel.com.

Cover photo: Dembinsky
Cover and book design: Alan G. Hartman

Library of Congress Cataloging-in-Publication Data
Classic sermons on the church/ Warren W. Wiersbe, compiler.
p. cm.— (Kregel classic sermons series)
Includes index.
1. Church—Sermons. 2. Sermons, American.
3. Sermons, English. 4. Sermons, English—Scotland.
I. Wiersbe, Warren W. II. Series.
BV603.C467 1998 262—dc21 97-41095
CIP

ISBN 0-8254-4081-5

Printed in the United States of America
1 2 3 / 04 03 02 01 00 99 98

CONTENTS

LIST OF SCRIPTURE TEXTS

PREFACE

THE *KREGEL CLASSIC SERMONS SERIES* is an attempt to assemble and publish meaningful sermons from master preachers about significant themes.

These are *sermons,* not essays or chapters taken from books about themes. Not all of these sermons could be called great, but all of them are *meaningful.* They apply the truths of the Bible to the needs of the human heart, which is something that all effective preaching must do.

While some are better known than others, all of the preachers whose sermons I have selected had important ministries and were highly respected in their day. The fact that a sermon is included in this volume does not mean that either the compiler or the publisher agrees with or endorses everything that the man did, preached, or wrote. The sermon is here because it has a valued contribution to make.

These are sermons about *significant* themes. The pulpit is no place to play with trivia. The preacher has thirty minutes in which to help mend broken hearts, change defeated lives, and save lost souls; he can never accomplish this demanding ministry by distributing homiletical tidbits. In these difficult days we do not need clever pulpiteers who discuss the times; we need dedicated ambassadors who will preach the eternities.

The reading of these sermons can enrich your spiritual life. The studying of them can enrich your skills as an interpreter and expounder of God's truth. However God uses these sermons in your life and ministry, my prayer is that His church around the world will be encouraged and strengthened by them.

WARREN W. WIERSBE

Meeting As a Congregation

Andrew A. Bonar (1810–1892) is perhaps best known as the friend and biographer of Robert Murray McCheyne and the brother of Horatius Bonar, Scotland's poet-preacher and author of over six hundred hymns. A minister of the Free Church of Scotland, Andrew Bonar emphasized the devotional life and was recognized for the depth of his prayer ministry. A zealous premillennialist, he had a keen interest in the plight of the Jews and, in 1839, accompanied McCheyne on an official ministerial commission to the Holy Land.

Andrew A. Bonar

1

MEETING AS A CONGREGATION

For where two or three are gathered together in my name, there am I in the midst of them (Matthew 18:20).

I BELIEVE YOU will find the origin of public worship in the book of Genesis, that book of beginnings. Enos, the son of Seth, was the first preacher and ministered to the first congregation, for so we understand the record, which says, "Then began men to call upon the name of the LORD" (4:26)—that is, they began to meet in public assemblies. It was the first of the happy companies whose gatherings together have been continued ever since. In the songs of Zion, special honor is accorded to those meetings of the saints: "The LORD loveth the gates of Zion more than all the dwellings of Jacob" (Ps. 87:2). The public assembly of His people on Mount Zion God loved more than all other gatherings because this was a loud proclamation of His name. He loved it all the more because these gathered ones met with their eyes on the altar and the atoning sacrifice. The sympathy, too, of such worshiping companies has always helped to give victory over selfishness. And the Lord gives more blessing when many are together than at other times, for this very end.

We sometimes hear people whose indolence and selfishness keep them at home say, "We are as well occupied at our own firesides on the Sabbath day as we would be in God's house." That cannot be true, since God has enjoined us not to forsake "the assembling of ourselves together" (Heb. 10:25). And it is very noticeable that when a man ceases to come to the house of God, you invariably find, as a result, that family worship has no longer a place in that home. And, too often, the worship of the closet languishes, even if it does not cease. In the sanctuary God has special blessings that we must lose when we forsake the assembling of ourselves together. God likes (we may say) to give His best blessings to more than one at a time on the lines of Ephesians 3:18: "with all saints." And while this is the Lord's rule, you will find also this to be true in your own experience that the blessing you get along with hundreds of others is far more plentiful and, perhaps, far deeper than what you get alone. Suppose a shower of rain falls only on you, it would give you some refreshment, no doubt. But if, at the same time, it soaks the ground all around you, making every tree and every blade of grass drop with moisture, and softens the ground all around, the coolness and the refreshing is wonderfully intensified. When God's people come thus together in the name of the Lord, the Lord makes this His special time for sending down a plentiful rain.

But now, let me ask you to notice in this passage (1) our presence together in Christ's name, and (2) Christ's presence with us when we are gathered together in His name.

Our Presence Together in Christ's Name

The Lord expected that in all after times His people would thus gather together. He takes it for granted that this shall be the case. The words, "Where two or three are gathered together in my name," take for granted that this is a practice that would never fail. We referred to Hebrews 10:25, but long before, in the book of Malachi, the Lord had made the gathering together of His people an ordinance: "Then they that feared the LORD spake often one to another [you can see that this is a gathering together in His name]: and the LORD hearkened" (3:16). Thus, God hearkened to what was going on in this meeting and marked down the attendance in His book of remembrance: "And they shall be mine, saith the LORD of hosts, in that day when I make up my jewels" (v. 17). In the Acts of the Apostles, and other passages, you will notice how continually the early Christians gathered together. Indeed, it is spoken of as a test of true discipleship: "They continued stedfastly in the apostles' doctrine and fellowship" (Acts 2:42). It was Christ Himself who, by His example and suggestions, introduced this meeting together among His own.

But you may say: "What is meant by 'in my name?'" It is not a mere gathering together in a meeting, for meetings may be convened for various purposes—social, political, or otherwise. It refers to none of these. The magnet that gathers this meeting is Christ's name. "When two or three are gathered together in my name." Think of what this name means. I refer to Malachi 3:16: "They that feared the LORD spake often one to another," and there you will find the Lord says, "A book of remembrance was written before him for them . . . that thought upon his name." The name of the Lord expresses the sum of God's perfections. In another of the prophets you have it said: "He shall stand and feed in the strength of the LORD, in the majesty of the name of the LORD his God" (Mic. 5:4)—in the name.

How can they meet "in the name of the LORD"? The meaning is this: We come together to think of the Lord—His perfection and all concerning Him. A congregation of true worshipers is a congregation of those who think upon His name. Often do we find the worshipers declaring, "We have thought of thy lovingkindness, O God, in the midst of thy temple. According to thy name, O God, so is thy praise unto the ends of the earth" (Ps. 48:9–10). At one time we are led to deep meditation on His lovingkindness as a part of His name, at another time of His holiness, at another of His justice—His determination to deal with unrighteousness in the way of vengeance. And then we stand still in amazement at the grace—the free love—that brings to us salvation. He has given us a Savior, and in that name "Jesus" (Jehovah who saves) is everything that enables us to approach the Holy One. You thus understand how meeting in the name implies that we stand in the sunshine of that name and bask in the bright rays that there fall on our souls.

Might I even put it this way? Our meeting together as Christians should be like that of Moses when the Lord came to him and put him in the cleft of the rock. His prayer went up: "I beseech thee, shew me thy glory" (Ex. 33:18). You prayed thus before you came together? And the Lord answered the prayer when the glory passed by, and His own voice proclaimed His own great and glorious name: "The LORD, The LORD [Jehovah, Jehovah] God, merciful and gracious, longsuffering, and abundant in goodness and truth, keeping mercy for thousands, forgiving iniquity and transgression and sin, and that will by no means clear the guilty" (34:6–7). We meet to hear the proclamation of that name from the Cross of Christ, where it is we find the full significance of the Master's words in John 17:6: "I have manifested thy name" (see also v. 26). Moses was so filled with adoring wonder and awe that he bowed his head toward the earth and worshiped. Blessed are we when our meeting together in that name affects us as it affected Moses. Are we not approaching at such a time the worship of the heavenly temple where they oftentimes fall down before the Lamb?

And if in the Old Testament days the worshipers found intense delight in gathering together, how much more should we in the fuller light of the Gospel? They longed, yes, fainted for the courts of the Lord. Their very hearts and flesh cried out for the living God who was to meet them there (see Ps. 84:2). Oh, with what joy they used to go up to the house of God "to give thanks unto the name of the LORD" (Ps. 122:4). Are you able every returning Lord's day to say, "I was glad when they said unto me, Let us go into the house of the LORD" (v. 1)?

Christ's Presence with Us When We Are Gathered Together in His Name

But I pass on, secondly, to speak of Christ's presence with those who have come together to enjoy the sunshine of His name. Our first and all-including loss by the Fall was loss of communion with God. But all we lost the Lord restores to us in redemption. All our gatherings together may afresh bring before us the restoration of this communion that we had lost. The Lord comes to meet us before we have come to meet Him. "Where two or three are gathered together in my name, there am I in the midst of them." Some may be here who have not found Him at home. We bring you good tidings. We tell you that it is His custom to reveal Himself to souls in the meeting of His saints. Our text declares: "Where two or three are gathered together in my name, there am I."

"There am I." The Lord Jesus meets those of His people who are thus gathered together in a special and peculiar manner, such as He is not in the habit to do in your retirement. He met Cephas, no doubt, alone after His resurrection (1 Cor. 15:5), but that was an exceptional case and not meant to be the same as meeting Him in the gathered assembly. It may be to such times of meeting that reference is made in the Song of Solomon, "Tell me, O thou whom my soul loveth, where thou feedest." And the answer is: "If thou know not . . . go thy way forth by the footsteps of the flock, and feed . . . beside the shepherds' tents" (1:7–8). Christ Himself has special delight and fellowship with us in such gatherings. The Shepherd likes to be in the midst of His flock. But what does He then do? He says, "There am I."

Let us ask what this implies—"there am I." There is an attraction in that announcement, surely. Even if He did nothing, it is something to be near Him. There is sunshine there, though He should never speak a word. Might I say, it is as when the mother's little ones find their enjoyment enhanced amazingly by the simple presence and smile of her who so loves them and whom they so love?

But more still is implied when He adds, "In the midst of them." It is as if He would say, "I am to be the very heart of the meeting and within the reach of all alike, not at one corner only." You often hear a needless addition made to this clause, "In the midst of them [to bless them and do them good]." Keep it as it stands; let the simple words speak without paraphrase or addition. There is (we said before) majesty and a strange attractiveness in this simple clause, "There am I." It is as when He came to His disciples saying, "It is I" (John 6:20). Notice the effect, the calm, the peace. "Immediately the ship was at the land" (v. 21). How divinely helpful, "I am there! I am there!" But always take in along with this, "in the midst of them." It suggests so much more: "I have come into the very center and heart of the meeting." No sooner has He overtaken the two disciples going to Emmaus than you can easily see that, as He walks between them and communes with them, quickly sadness gives way to secret joy until their hearts burn within them. And we go up to the throne and observe, in the book of Revelation, the position He is accustomed to taking. If we find Him "who walketh in the midst of the seven golden candlesticks" (2:1), then at another time He is "the Lamb which is in the midst of the throne" (7:17), the heavenly companies all gathered around Him!

Perhaps for this, among other reasons, that visit is fully recorded in John 20:19 as a sample of what might be expected at such gatherings. He came to the Upper Room. Notice in passing, nobody heard the door open. Nobody, to this hour, knows how He got into the Upper Room. The disciples were met together in His name to talk about Him and to think about Him, and the doors were fast closed and barred. But all at once they found Jesus standing in the midst. For it is silently He comes in among us, unseen, and all at once we find that He is here! On that same occasion His first word was, "Peace be unto you," showing them His hands that spoke of the cross and pointing to His side that was pierced. Is it not just thus that He wishes us to be ever blessed when we are gathered in His name? He begins by speaking peace to our souls, peace through the blood of the Cross, peace through His pierced hands and side. You need never gather in His name without receiving a fresh view of the blood of Christ that gives peace to the soul. Pray for your pastor, that he may never, to the day of his death, preach a single sermon or be with you in any gathering together in His name without pointing you to the blood shed for the remission of sin.

But there is still more here. After He had thus spoken and led them anew to the source of true peace, "He breathed on them, and saith unto them, Receive ye the Holy Ghost" (v. 22). When you gather together as a congregation, let me ask, Do you expect to receive the Holy Spirit? Perhaps you reply, "If we are believers, have not we the Holy Spirit already?" The Holy Spirit is in you as the water in a well, but the well may be very far sunk down and so you need to cry, "Spring up, O well" (Num. 21:17). And every time you come together in the house of God you have special reason for expecting the springing up of this well, for you have this promise and can hold it up to the Lord: "If ye then, being evil, know how to give good gifts unto your children, how much more shall your Father which is in heaven give good things [the Holy Spirit] to them that ask Him?" (Matt. 7:11; see Luke 11:13). A father gives to his little children not once or twice only, but from day to day and likes to have them continually coming. Even so, disciples who have the Spirit already come to get greater communications of the same Spirit. See that you always come up in the expectation of receiving the eye salve to enable you to see more clearly, to get more from Christ's fullness of the fruit of the Spirit—"love, joy, peace, longsuffering, gentleness, goodness, faith, meekness, temperance" (Gal. 5:22–23), and the like.

But even this is not all. He added, when breathing the Spirit upon them, "As my Father hath sent me, even so send I you" (John 20:21). Go away now and tell others about salvation and the Savior. Go and spread the tidings to all men of peace by the Savior's work: "The chastisement of our peace was upon him" (Isa. 53:5). Yes, remember every time we come together and as we go hence: "As my Father hath sent me, even so send I you" to spread the tidings that have brought peace to your own souls. Sit not down in selfish enjoyment when your hearts are burning within you after some fresh discovery of the riches of grace in John 3:16: "God so loved the world, that he gave his only begotten Son, that whosoever believeth in him should not perish, but have everlasting life." Go and tell men these same tidings. And if more were needed to induce you to do so, this might be added, namely, in the very act of telling your fellowman of this salvation you yourself get immense gain. In a word, if you would have your sanctification carried on, if you would have your own communion perfected, go forth with these words ringing in your ears: "As my Father hath sent me, even so send I you."

Come together, then, for these ends. In Revelation you see how Christ sends messages to the churches, His gathered ones that meet in His name. But they always meet with the ulterior view of their giving to others the water of life that they themselves have been tasting. Oh, dear people, let us seek to have more profitable meetings than we have ever had. Let us seek to get a fresh start today in this direction. How much of this kind of gathering together shall there be? Will you every Sabbath drink of this well and run with its living waters to others? It is not eloquence nor intellectual effort that the Holy Spirit delights to use; it is the preaching of "peace through the blood of his cross" (Col. 1:20). Let us, in this way, seek conversion in all our meetings, in our Sunday schools, and wherever souls can be dealt with. Oh, let there be none here merely sitting on the steps of the ark, liking to hear that the door is still open—sitting, we say, on the steps but not within and so in danger every moment, for the door may be shut and the flood sweep them away. Shall the ark of salvation stand open while you will not cross the threshold? Who among us are merely formalists? You are so if you do not gather together in Christ's name. You are mere formalists if you cannot truly sing that psalm in which we declare: "One thing have I desired of the LORD, that will I seek after; that I may dwell in the house of the LORD all the days of my life, to behold the beauty of the LORD, and to inquire in his temple" (Ps. 27:4). You are mere formalists if not meeting with Christ, though you come to the meeting place. But when you come with the full purpose and positive desire to behold the beauty of the Lord, then you may expect a meeting with Christ.

From 1 Corinthians 14:23–25, we see that occurrences like the following often took place in the early church: A hearer not in Christ would drop in, perhaps from mere curiosity, knowing that it was a gathering of those who met in Christ's name. He sees that the worshipers are truly devout and are seeking the Lord in downright earnestness. He sees that they listen with eagerness to the word spoken and that they pray and sing with the soul and the heart. He may not know that that overpowering conviction that seizes on his soul proceeds from the presence of that Christ who said, "There am I in the midst." But so it is. This Zaccheus-hearer falls down and worships and goes home to report, "God is in [them] of a truth" (v. 25). Oh, is there convincing and convicting work in our meetings? Are there such prayers and praises, such intense feelings, that even a careless one, hearing what is spoken and listening to the prayers and to the songs of praise, is overawed in his inmost soul? Will you, henceforth, more than ever, aim at having such results in our congregational meetings? Oh, we should every week expect and bespeak His blessing. If the Lord is present, every gathering will be a memorable one because from our gathering together there will be tidings carried up to heaven that will create new joy in heaven over at least one sinner repenting. And look forward. Oh, for that eternal meeting, Forever with the Lord! "The Lamb which is in the midst of the throne" (Rev. 7:17). Oh, when shall it come!

What Happened at Pentecost?

Clovis Gillham Chappell (1882–1972) was one of American Methodism's best-known and most effective preachers. He pastored churches in Washington, D.C.; Dallas and Houston, Texas; Memphis, Tennessee; and Birmingham, Alabama; and his pulpit ministry drew great crowds. He was especially known for his biographical sermons that made biblical figures live and speak to our modern day. He published about thirty volumes of sermons.

This message was taken from *Evangelistic Sermons of Clovis G. Chappell,* published by Abingdon Press in 1965.

Clovis Gillham Chappell

2

WHAT HAPPENED AT PENTECOST?

What meaneth this? (Acts 2:12).

PENTECOST IS THE GREATEST EVENT in the history of the Christian church. But, in spite of this, I am persuaded that for many earnest people it has little or no meaning. Some have become so mystified by that about it which is passing and nonessential that they have missed what is essential and abiding. Therefore, instead of fixing our minds upon the events of this story that we confessedly do not understand, let us think of that about it which we cannot help but understand. Let us forget for the moment the fiery tongues and the rushing wind and think of the change that this experience, whatever its nature, wrought in the disciples themselves. Having considered what this experience did for these friends of Jesus, we may be able to better judge what that experience was.

What Did Pentecost Do for the Disciples?

What did Pentecost do for the disciples? *It welded them into a brotherhood*. Any close reading of the Gospels will reveal the fact that one chief purpose of Jesus was to build a brotherhood. "By this," He said, "shall all men know that ye are my disciples, if ye have love one to another" (John 13:35). He recognized that there were two types of personalities in the world—one made for hate, the other for love. One works toward the dividing of men, the other toward the uniting of them. He claimed that He Himself was a uniting force. He claimed further that all who were engaged with Him in the building of men into a brotherhood were His friends and that all others were His enemies: "He that is not with me is against me; and he that gathereth not with me scattereth abroad"

(Matt. 12:30). His purpose, therefore, was the building of a brotherhood.

But, in spite of the fact that Jesus gave His energies wholeheartedly to this high task, at the time of His death He seems to have made but little progress. He had gathered about Him an inner circle of twelve men. But while these were outwardly one, inwardly they were far from being united. It is at once distressing and depressing to realize that they went in to their last meal with their Master spitting hot words at each other as they wrangled over the old question as to who should be greatest in the kingdom. It was the Master Himself who had to assume the role of a slave and wash His disciples' feet. Not one of them was brotherly enough to undertake this lowly task. But for Pentecost, this little organization would doubtless have melted like a rope of sand.

But after this experience in the Upper Room, Dr. Luke could say, "The multitude of them that believed were of one heart and of one soul" (Acts 4:32). This oneness belonged to the original group that had been friends of Jesus before His crucifixion. Into it had been brought orthodox Jews of the homeland. Into it had also been brought foreign-born Jews, from whom those of the homeland had been separated by a wide chasm. Into this brotherhood came, a little later, despised Samaritans and Gentiles. Thus men and women of different races and nationalities, of widely different social standing, were brought together in the bonds of a common brotherhood.

So close were these ties that those who had once been far apart worshiped and took communion together. Not only so, but at first they shared their material substance: "Neither said any of them that ought of the things which he possessed was his own; but they had all things common" (v. 32). This is the nearest approach to Christian communism that we find in the New Testament. It was a communism of spending, not of earning. As to detail it was imperfect. But the spirit that prompted it was an altogether right spirit. It was a spirit of brotherliness.

It was this devotion of one Christian to another, this spirit of brotherliness, that was one of the most impressive characteristics of the early church. The pagan world looked on these little "colonies of heaven" with wistful wonder. "How these Christians love each other!" they said in amazement. And, because they wanted to love and be loved, they were drawn into these little groups. To this day there is nothing quite so impressive as a church that is a brotherhood. It is equally true that there is nothing that more grossly misrepresents our Lord than a church that is torn by strife and discord. Let the membership of any church get to fighting among themselves and the Devil may take a holiday so far as that church is concerned. Pentecost welded the friends of Jesus into a brotherhood.

Then, through this experience, *these disciples became literally obsessed by a passion for witnessing*. They had an irresistible urge to share their experience with their fellows. No sooner had the multitude come together saying, "What meaneth this?" than Simon Peter was ready with an answer. He stood up with the Eleven, Luke tells us. There was one spokesman, but every member of the group bore his testimony by standing up with the spokesman. One weakness of much of our modern witnessing is that so often the present-day Simon must stand up without the Eleven. Those that should be there to back his testimony, to give it pungency and power, are not present. Simon Peter, with the backing of his fellow saints, so testified that men were cut to the heart, and some three thousand were brought into the church.

A few days later Simon Peter, with John, is on his way to prayer meeting. At the gate of the temple, he is met by a professional beggar. This man asks for alms. Neither Peter nor John has any money, but they do have a passion to share their experience. Therefore, Simon preaches to this professional panhandler with the same hot enthusiasm that he has preached to the vast multitude. Not only so, but he preaches effectively. There is a new face at prayer meeting that day. This beggar is changed into a giver. He enters with Simon and John into the temple, "walking, and leaping, and praising God" (3:8).

Other days have passed, and these two apostles have clashed with the authorities and are under arrest. These authorities are a bit at a loss to know what to do with them. But at last one offers this happy suggestion: "Let us straitly threaten them, that they speak henceforth to no man in this name" (4:17). Therefore, they call Simon Peter and John and command them "not to speak at all nor teach in the name of Jesus" (v. 18). But Peter and John answer and say, "Whether it be right in the sight of God to hearken unto you more than unto God, judge ye. For we cannot but speak the things which we have seen and heard" (vv. 19–20). Silence, they maintain, is for them an utter impossibility. They can no more cease from speaking than the grass can cease from growing green at the kiss of the springtime.

That these disciples were speaking only sober truth is evidenced by the rebuke of the authorities when they are again put under arrest. Listen to what they say. These authorities seem full of righteous indignation. "We commanded you not to teach nor to speak at all in the name of Jesus, and you have filled all Jerusalem with your teaching" (5:28, paraphrased). How amazing! Among those that had heard the message were foreign-born Jews who were visiting in Jerusalem. One of them was a brilliant young chap by the name of Stephen. He at once came to be possessed by the same passion for telling his story. He witnessed with such power that his hearers, unable to resist his words with logic, resorted to stones. In fact, they dragged him outside the city and mobbed him.

Then what happened? It was now evident that to witness was dangerous. They could not do so except at the risk of personal danger. "Therefore," the story continues with strangest logic, "they that were scattered abroad went every where preaching the word" (8:4). Thus, when these authorities sought to put out the holy fire that Pentecost had kindled, they failed utterly. Instead of putting it out, they only scattered it. Thus, by and by, the whole Roman world was set on fire. This was done not by preaching from the pulpit but by the testimony of nameless nobodies who laid almost violent hands on every chance passerby to tell him of the amazing happenings that had taken place in their own lives and in those of their fellows. Pentecost gave to the friends of Jesus a passion for witnessing.

This experience also gave to the disciples an incredible joy and hopefulness and courage that fill us with wistful wonder to this hour. The very first impression they made upon outsiders was that theirs was the joy of the intoxicated. "These men are full of new wine" (2:13) was the easy explanation. Most of us know how a mild form of intoxication banishes the gloom, changes sadness into gladness, timidity into courage, and want into wealth. There is a classic Tennessee story of a poverty-stricken brother who met a friend that was on the point of moving to Texas. "I have a brother in Texas," he informed his friend. "I want you to tell him for me that my crops have failed, my hogs have died. Unless he helps me, I don't see how I can get through the winter." But a boon companion immensely cheered this impoverished man from his flask. Therefore, when he again met his friend an hour or so later, he merely said, "I have a brother in Texas. If you see him, tell him that if he needs anything just to let me know."

This absurd joyousness seems to have been born, at least in part, of the mad certainty of these disciples that they were sure to win. They believed that the kingdoms of this world were actually going to become the kingdoms of our Lord and of His Christ. In this mad faith, they faced stark impossibilities with holy laughter. They encountered the most deadly dangers unafraid. Opposed, arrested, publicly whipped, they knew neither discouragement nor resentment. They, rather, rejoiced that they were counted worthy to suffer shame for the sake of their victorious Lord. Thus, they lived in joyous expectancy. They were possessed by a boundless optimism and a dauntless courage that were all but irresistible.

Finally, *this experience brought to these disciples amazing power*. In fact, it enabled them to do what any sane man would have said was flatly impossible. Suppose one had said to a spectator who saw that little prayer meeting crowd of 120, on the way to the Upper Room, in the temple, "There moves a group that is going to shake this entire city. They are going to shake the whole Jewish nation. They are going to shake the whole Roman world. Age-old abuses like infanticide and slavery are going to vanish before them. They are going to breathe on all the subsequent centuries like a spiritual springtime." Who would have believed it? "Impossible!" any sane man would have said. Yet, history declares that this actually did happen.

What Did Pentecost Do for the Church?

This, then, is the effect of Pentecost on the church: a brotherly church, a church with a passion for witnessing, a church with a joyous optimism and a dauntless courage, a church with amazing power. What was the cause? How did this group of believers come to be this kind of church?

Suppose we listen to the testimony of those who were present and who participated in this great event. They explain the change that had been wrought in themselves in terms of the Divine. They use varied words to express this conviction, but it all adds up to this: they have not simply come upon new evidences of God or of the resurrection of Jesus; they have, rather, come to a new and compelling awareness of God Himself. They have come to realize beyond a peradventure that the Christ who was crucified is really alive. Not only so, He is both with and within them, individually. He is also among them as a group. They know that in giving the Holy Spirit, God has given Himself. Thus they tell us that the change that has been wrought in them has been wrought by God and God alone.

It is my conviction that their testimony is true. I believe this because no other explanation will satisfy. We simply cannot account for what these ordinary men and women became and what they did in any other way. Then, I believe that their explanation is correct because it really does explain. They became the kind of men and women, and did the kind of work, that I would expect

God-possessed men and women to become and to do. After this experience they ceased to imitate Christ painstakingly and came to reproduce Him spontaneously. They sing with Paul, "For to me to live is Christ" (Phil. 1:21), and "I am crucified with Christ: nevertheless, I live; yet not I, but Christ liveth in me" (Gal. 2:20). Should I say, "Tennyson lives in me," you would expect me to sing in some fashion as Tennyson sang. These people, claiming to be indwelled of Christ, went out to live even as He lived.

Look, for instance, at this picture. Here is a man, brilliant, gifted, possessed by that love of life that belongs to young manhood at its best. Yet, this young man, Stephen by name, meets an untimely death. Because he dares to speak his deepest convictions, he is dragged without the city gates and cruelly mobbed. But he dies without bitterness, and there is a light upon his face that was never seen on land or sea. As he falls asleep, he prays this prayer: "Lord, lay not this sin to their charge" (Acts 7:60). That marks him as a close kinsman to Him who, when hung on the cross, prayed thus for His enemies: "Father, forgive them; for they know not what they do" (Luke 23:34). We cannot account for such lives except in terms of God.

Just as we cannot account for what these men became apart from God, no more can we account for what they accomplished. They were without social standing. They were without wealth. They did not have enough influence to avoid the whipping post and the jail, the arena and the stake. Yet they turned the world upside down. But they never think of these mighty changes as wrought by themselves. "Do not look on us," Simon Peter warns, "as if by our own power or holiness we had done this. God has thus glorified His servant Jesus" (Acts 3:12–13, paraphrased). And always, when Paul reports the results of his missionary efforts, it is not what he and his fellows have accomplished but what God has done through them. They could no more have accomplished what they did accomplish apart from this experience of God than a drop of water could change the Sahara Desert into a flower garden. This is the only explanation that really explains.

What Does Pentecost Mean for Us?

What does Pentecost mean for us? It means that this same transforming and empowering experience of God is for you and me. This is the testimony of Simon Peter as he spoke on that distant day: "The promise is unto you, and to your children, and to all that are afar off, even as many as the Lord our God shall call" (2:39). This is to be the experience not of the exceptional Christian but of all Christians. It is an experience that is perfectly normal. Any other is subnormal. Nothing is more evident than that our Lord never intended that you and I should carry on in the energy of the flesh. Through our very failures, He is saying to us what He said in the long ago: "Without me ye can do nothing" (John 15:5). It is only in and through Him that we can become and do our best.

It is, therefore, highly reasonable that the experience that made these early saints what they were should be available for us. Certainly there was never a greater need for a God who is able to do exceedingly abundantly above all that we can ask or think than there is today. Only God can enable us to save a civilization that threatens to collapse into an abysm of blood and tears through unbrotherly hate. If there is not a power that can remake us and equip us for the task of building the kingdom of God, then I see no hope for our world.

If, then, this experience is available for us, how can we enter upon it? How do we avail ourselves of that mighty power called electricity? We do so by discovering the laws of electricity and being obedient to them. It is thus that we avail ourselves of the power of God. "We are his witnesses of these things; and so is also the Holy Ghost, whom God hath given to them that obey him" (Acts 5:32). As the room is flooded with sunshine when the blinds are lifted, so our lives are flooded by His presence when we open the door for His incoming. He is not merchandise to be bought. He is a gift to be received: "Of his fulness have all we received" (John 1:16).

On the farm where I spent my boyhood, under the deep shade of beech and oak trees, there is a great, flat rock. Upon the face of this rock, hands that have doubtless been dust for centuries once chiseled a basin. In spite of the fact that this basin is as lifeless as death, it sings and prattles with one of the most luxurious springs that a thirsty man ever kissed upon the lips. Go to this spring in the dead of winter or in the noontide hush of midsummer, and you will find it prattling and laughing like a happy child. How is it that this basin offers its life-giving cup to every passerby through all the changing years? In answer to this question, the basin can only point to the majestic hill that towers in the background and say, "Of its fullness have I received." It is such receiving that makes the finest of giving possible for us. "If any man thirst, let him come unto me, and drink. He that believeth on me, as the scripture hath said, out of his [inner life] shall flow rivers of living water. (But this spake he of the Spirit, which they that believe on him should receive)" (John 7:37–39).

The Lord's Counsel for the Church of Today

William Culbertson (1905–1971) was born and educated in Philadelphia and was identified all of his ministry with the Reformed Episcopal Church of America. He pastored churches in Pennsylvania and New Jersey and in 1937 was elected bishop of the New York and Philadelphia Synod. In 1942, he became dean of education at the Moody Bible Institute in Chicago and in 1947 was named acting president, upon the death of Will H. Houghton. In 1948, he became president of the school, a position he held with distinction until 1971, when he was named chancellor. "My first impression and the lasting one," said Dr. Wilbur M. Smith, "is that he is a man of God." He was in great demand as a preacher and widely recognized as a leader in Christian education.

This sermon was taken from the compilation of his Moody Bible Institute "Founder's Week" messages, *The Faith Once Delivered,* published in 1972 by Moody Press, and is used by permission.

William Culbertson

3

THE LORD'S COUNSEL FOR THE CHURCH OF TODAY

Revelation 3:14–22

THE CHURCH TODAY, despite its largeness and its ability to exert pressure and its tacit acceptance by world leaders, finds itself without real authority. It is all very well for those of us who are fundamental in doctrine to blame the modernists for this situation, and that there is such blame to be attached to liberal theology is not to be denied. It is all very well for us to castigate the liberal and to censure those who will not bow to the Word of God. But sober reflection will remind us that even among us in the homeland there is no Nathan to stand in the portals of government and thunder God's condemnation of sin; there is no Elijah who elicits the threats of an angry, ungodly ruler; there is no John the Baptist who would rather lose his head than his crown; there is no Martin Luther who is the recognized leader of God's people; there is no John Knox to live and pray consternation and fear into the heart of a queen; there is no apparent Wesley and no apparent Whitefield to wear out for God. A surfeited, cynical, yet fearful world looks at all our machinery and all our bricks and mortar and all our gadgets and devices, and is utterly unimpressed.

You say the world is sin-hardened; it is far from God; it is beyond reach. Let me ask the simple question: Is it? Can it be harder to reach, considering the few available to reach it, than the world in which the apostles lived? Is anything too hard for the Lord? No; the trouble is with us. And I think, yes, I know, that God would have us turn

---

Unless otherwise indicated, all Scripture in this sermon is quoted from the *American Standard Version* of 1901.

from looking for others to blame and look into our own hearts to discover the real reason for the situation in which we find ourselves.

The Gospel has still its ancient power. As a matter of fact, God is waiting for us to do something. You know, surely you do, that God always begins with the leaders. He's waiting for us—I'm speaking particularly to the ministers, to the missionaries, to the Christian workers in attendance upon this conference—God is waiting for us to make a move toward Him and toward His will.

I speak as a dispensational, pretribulational premillenarian. I speak as one who is familiar with the interpretation of Revelation 2 and 3 according to the above view. Why should we not turn to what the Lord counsels the Laodicean church? We believe we are living in the days of the Laodicean church. But wait a moment. Too long we've been casting our eyes around to find the evidences of what is said of the Laodicean church outside ourselves. It is about time we begin to look inside. Can we shake ourselves loose from our complacency, our unwillingness to face reality, long enough to take an objective look at our own condition?

God has been speaking scathingly to my own soul from this Laodicean epistle, and I must admit that the look God has given me into my own profession has not been a pleasant one. I wonder if you will dare to put your life alongside the description the Lord Jesus Christ makes of this church and discover whether or not certain of its faults are not to be found in you? It may make some of us realize that we've been inoculated with just enough Christianity to immunize ourselves from the real thing. But if we'll dare to look and dare to listen—and God helps us to realize our desperate condition—then thank God we can do something about it with His help.

God always goes to the heart of a matter. He does so in this little letter given by the risen, ascended Lord through John to the church. Here is no pep talk; here is no challenge, in the much-abused use of that word today; here is no touching of things on the periphery. The Lord strikes at the root of the trouble. If my study has led me to understand the basic need of those described in this epistle, I find it in three words in 3:17—*poor, blind, naked*.

Will you notice that these three characteristics, these three conditions, are those that the Lord lays hold of in verse 18. He says, "I counsel thee to buy of me gold refined by fire, that thou mayest become rich; and [buy of me] white garments, that thou mayest clothe thyself, and that the shame of thy nakedness be not made manifest; and [buy of me] eyesalve to anoint thine eyes, that thou mayest see." Poor, blind, naked! "Buy of me gold; buy of me eyesalve; buy of me white garments." I want to talk to you about this business of buying gold, buying eye salve, and buying white garments.

"Buy of Me Gold": Sacrifice

First of all I want to talk about heavenly currency—gold refined in the fire. The Lord is not talking about the gold of this world but the gold of the world to come. What is the currency that is used in the world to come? What will make us rich in the world to come? Let us listen to our Lord and Savior Jesus Christ. In Matthew 5:10–12: "Blessed are they that have been persecuted for righteousness' sake: for theirs is the kingdom of heaven. Blessed are ye when men shall reproach you, and persecute you, and say all manner of evil against you falsely, for my sake. Rejoice, and be exceeding glad: for great is your reward in heaven: for so persecuted they the prophets that were before you."

Then Matthew 6:19–21: "Lay not up for yourselves treasures upon the earth, where moth and rust consume, and where thieves break through and steal: but lay up for yourselves treasures in heaven, where neither moth nor rust doth consume, and where thieves do not break through nor steal: for where thy treasure is, there will thy heart be also."

Matthew 19:27–29: "Then answered Peter and said unto him, Lo, we have left all, and followed thee; what then shall we have? And Jesus said unto them, Verily I say unto you, that ye who have followed me, in the regeneration when the Son of man shall sit on the throne of his glory, ye also shall sit upon twelve thrones, judging the twelve tribes of Israel. And every one that hath left houses, or brethren, or sisters, or father, or mother, or children, or lands, for my name's sake, shall receive a hundredfold, and shall inherit eternal life."

Luke 12:21, the end of the story about the true treasure: "So is he that layeth up treasure for himself, and is not rich toward God."

Now I am sure there are other ways of expressing it, there may be other emphases that you may think of, but frankly I believe that this world's equivalent to the gold of heaven is sacrifice on the part of the child of God. It seems to me that these verses, which we have read, from the Lord Jesus permit no alternative. If we are persecuted, if we suffer, we'll be rewarded. If we leave houses and loved ones and friends for Christ, we'll be rewarded.

There is a heavenly currency that our Lord speaks of here in Revelation 3 as refined in the fire—sacrifice. The basis of sacrifice is willingness to suffer, to die to self and to the world, and it all results in an utter transformation of a sense of values. When one comes to the place of discipleship and in consecration yields himself to the Lord for His will, things that once mattered no longer matter, and things that were once important are no longer important. All of life is different. "Buy of me gold refined by fire." Sacrifice!

Where is the spirit of sacrifice among us? As I've gone about, on occasion I've seen this principle demonstrated, and my heart has been humbled and my soul has been refreshed as I have noticed the utter dedication of some of the children of God; but alas and alack, I see very little of it. Every once in a while I have to stop and say, "Culbertson, what are you living for? How much is it costing you to be a disciple of the Lord?" For there is always the subtle temptation to beguile ourselves and to seek the way of ease and of comfort. We don't want to sacrifice.

Whatever this word to the Laodiceans may mean to those who are not Christians, there is this word for us, and God help us to face it. The Lord Jesus looks at you and at me and says, "You're poor! You're poor!" Oh, He doesn't say we're poor as far as this world's goods are concerned, for most of us have more than we need. But so far as the exchequer of heaven is concerned and the coinage of the Celestial City, we're abysmally poor, for there's no sacrifice in our faith. If we can take it easy, if we can retain our respectability and be well thought of by our comrades, that's all that concerns us. But real sacrifice astounds us and frightens us, and we're liable to say that the one who makes sacrifices is utterly beside himself and foolish. So little are we committed to what we say we believe!

I venture to say that there is not one fundamental, orthodox Christian hearing my voice tonight who does not acknowledge at once that we lose what we keep or spend on ourselves. With our lips we pay tribute to the dictum that we must give to gain and that what we grasp we lose. But are we living it? Enough of this business of mouthing out platitudes! How much does it cost you? How much does it cost me?

Go into the realm of time. We pat ourselves on our backs and say, "We give time to the Lord." But alongside of the time that we give to ourselves, it's a pittance, and so often it's the leftovers we give the Lord.

And what about this matter of money? I know there are those who are giving, and giving sacrificially. But the number giving that way are a paltry few alongside the number who claim to be fundamental Christians. Too long a few have been bearing the burden of the many, and the reputation that we have of giving to our local churches and to missions and to institutions like Moody Bible Institute we've earned at the expense of a few souls whom only God knows. God will reward them in the coming day—the rest of us will stand there with our hands and our hearts empty.

And what about our strength? God has to talk to me about this. I'm far from perfect, but I thank God I live close enough to Him to hear Him once in a while, and I get ashamed of myself. The subtle temptation is always to take it easy, and somehow our friends help us out.

They tell us that we're working too hard. Now, there are a few—I'm not speaking against them, noble souls they are—who say when you tell them to take it easy, "Man, how can I take it easy?" The rest of us are just waiting for the word so that we have some excuse to slink down into indolence and idle our time away.

"I counsel thee to buy of me gold refined by fire"—something that is going to last beyond the things of time and space. Too long I've been applying this Laodicean epistle to the lukewarm church members whom I see on all sides, and in pride I have been saying I'm all right and it doesn't touch me, when as a matter of fact it touches me first of all.

Mark it, Christian leader; mark it, pastor. Until it touches you, it won't touch anybody to whom you minister. I haven't learned very much, but one thing I have learned, that if I minister to people, God ministers to them about the same thing He has to talk to me about. And until He has talked to me about it, it is just clanging cymbals and empty words.

"I counsel thee to buy of me gold." Oh, my friend, is the Spirit of God beginning to speak to your heart? Don't shut Him out. Let Him begin to search, let Him begin to lay hold on these cold hearts of ours and stir us from our lethargy.

Concerning this matter of heavenly currency, I'd like to tell you a story I read several years ago, but I'd like to take the privilege of telling it in the first person, even though it was not my experience.

I saw in a dream that I was in the Celestial City, though when and how I was transmitted there I could not tell. I was one of the great multitude that no man could number, from all countries and peoples and times and ages.

Somehow I found myself standing next to a man who had been in heaven for two thousand years. "Who are you?" I said to him. We understood each other, for we both spoke the heavenly language.

"I," said he, "was a Roman Christian. I was one who died in Nero's persecutions. They covered me with pitch and fastened me to a stake and set me on fire to light up Nero's gardens."

"How awful!" I exclaimed.

"No, no," said he, "I was glad to do something for the Lord Jesus. He died on the cross for me."

The man on the other side then spoke. "I've been in heaven only a few hundred years. I came from an island in the South Seas, Erromanga. John Williams, a missionary, came and told me about the Lord Jesus, and I learned to love Him. My fellow countrymen killed the missionary, and they caught and bound me. I was beaten until I fainted and they thought I was dead, but I revived. The next day they came and took off my head and cooked my body and ate it."

"Oh, how terrible!" I exclaimed.

"No," he answered, "I was glad to die a Christian. You see, the missionaries had told me that the Lord Jesus was scourged and crowned with thorns for me."

Then they turned to me and said, "What did you suffer for Him? Did you sell what you had and with the money send men like John Williams to tell the heathen about the Lord Jesus?" I was speechless. And while they were both looking at me I awoke. It was a dream. But I lay on my soft bed for hours thinking of the money I had wasted on my own pleasures, on my extra clothing, on my many luxuries, and I realized that I did not know what the words of the Lord Jesus meant, "If any man would come after me, let him deny himself, and take up his cross, and follow me" (Matt. 16:24).

What do you know of that? The Lord Jesus looked at the Laodicean church and said, "You are poor."

I look in my heart and say, "It's so, it's so!"

"Buy of me gold." You have the opportunity, and in all the strength of your new life in Christ Jesus you may stand tonight and be a disciple. Buy gold for heaven.

"Buy of Me Eyesalve": Vision

It is not necessary to take a great deal of time to develop the thought, but, as a matter of fact, we are blind. I will admit at once that the Christian who is born of the

Holy Spirit is not totally blind. Once I was blind, but now I see. Thank God, there is some vision, but we are limiting God and coming short of God's purpose because we have defective vision.

Let me read 2 Peter 1:9: "For he that lacketh these things is blind, seeing only what is near, having forgotten the cleansing from his old sins." That's the trouble: seeing only what is near. If there is one malady above another that plagues Christians, it is this business of nearsightedness. We're living for the things of time and sense. Our eyes have not become accustomed to looking beyond the horizon into the Celestial City; the world is too much with us. Unfortunately, in these days when the Devil is so active, the world is more and more with us who claim to be separated Christians.

Seeing only what is near—what about that, my friends? It is so easy to be engrossed in our own concerns, in our own lives, in our own families that our hearts don't beat in sympathy and compassion and love for others. It takes a sledgehammer blow from God even to dislodge us a portion of an inch from our complacency, our self-satisfaction, our comfort and our ease.

Let me read 2 Corinthians 4:18: "We look not at the things which are seen, but at the things which are not seen: for the things which are seen are temporal; but the things which are not seen are eternal." Are you looking at eternal things tonight? If you are, it will affect the way you live. You may sing about them, you may claim them, you may testify to them, but unless you have your eyes set on eternity, you are singing and testifying and speaking a lie.

God help us to start to mean business with Him. Too long we've had the right phrase on our lips, but our hearts have been empty and cold. Our disobedience speaks more effectively of our disregard for the Lord than all our pious singing of hymns of praise, which only outwardly set forth our devotion. Yes, God help us to acknowledge His deity. But the acknowledgment of His deity, if it is a true acknowledgment, will make a difference in your fealty to Him right now. Don't talk to me and don't fight about this business of the Lord being Lord when you're denying it in the way you live. It's about time we get the two things together. If our doctrine is right and held in our hearts, it will make our lives right.

"[Buy of me] eyesalve." Where are you going to get this eye salve? Peter tells you. You've forgotten something, you've forgotten your cleansing from your old sins. Listen, if you're nearsighted and you have no heart of compassion for a world that is lost, no concern for others, you need to get back to the Cross. You need to get back to that place where the wonder of it all dawned on your soul until it overwhelmed you and in gratitude you lisped your praise to God, and nothing that He asked was too much, no command that He uttered was too great. You need some eye salve tonight. I know you do; I need it too.

How about it, pastor? You're shut up to that little work. It's a good work, God bless you in it. But does the sun rise and set on it, and is that all there is? God help you. Is your own denomination the start and the finish? Is it? I have a right to ask this, for I am a member of a denomination; I'm an official in it. But, my friend, are we so nearsighted that we don't see the onmarch of the purposes of God in the whole church? God has left us here to see to it that by life and by lip we get the message of God to the ends of the earth.

I'll be frank with you, one of the reasons I came to Moody Bible Institute was that under God and with His blessing I felt I could have a bigger part in the march of missions to the ends of the earth by touching young people. That's the only reason I gave up the position I had in the east. I'm here because I believe God is doing something and I want to be in the march.

I want a vision, a vision that goes beyond my own kith and kin, beyond my own colleagues, a vision that embraces the world. How the Lord Jesus has broken my heart with His word in the gospel of John: "Other sheep I have, which are not of this fold: them also I *must* bring" (10:16, emphasis added). Oh, do you catch it? Our hearts should miss a beat if this is what He's doing. Are you nearsighted tonight? Buy eye salve of Him.

"Buy of Me White Garments": Character

Now, this is not the garment of salvation, let us get that straight. You're going to buy these garments. In Revelation 19 there is an important word about garments: "The marriage of the Lamb is come, and his wife hath made herself ready" (v. 7). Now look at verse 8: "And it was given unto her that she should array herself in fine linen, bright and pure: for the fine linen is the righteous acts of the saints." Many of you have thought that John by the Holy Spirit was talking about the imputed righteousness of Christ. No, the *American Standard Version* is absolutely correct; it's another Greek word. It's the righteous acts of the saints, and they are the garments you buy—white garments.

Recently, in teaching from the book of Hebrews God searched my own heart very deeply. In Hebrews 1:9 we read: "Thou [that is, the Lord Jesus] hast loved righteousness, and hated iniquity; therefore God, thy God, hath anointed thee with the oil of gladness above thy fellows." Perhaps it will surprise you that the word that gripped my soul and reduced me to dust and ashes before God was the word "fellows." I think the reason I hadn't caught it before was because the word *fellows,* in my mind, had another connotation. I'm going to change that word, and I have justification for the change. Let me put it this way and I believe God may speak to you about it the way He spoke to me: "Therefore God, thy God, hath anointed thee with the oil of gladness above thy companions."

Do you know that the Lord Jesus has companions? Moses had a Joshua, David had a Hushai, Rehoboam had the young men who were around him; a king had companions, those who were close to him. The Lord Jesus is anointed with the oil of gladness above His companions. Who are these companions? Turn back to Revelation 3:4–5: "But thou hast a few names in Sardis that did not defile their garments: and they shall walk with me in white; for they are worthy. He that overcometh shall thus be arrayed in white garments; and I will in no wise blot his name out of the book of life, and I will confess his name before my Father, and before his angels."

When He shall come resplendent in His glory,
To take His own from out this vale of night,
O may I know the joy of His appearing,
Only at morn to walk with Him in white.

When I shall stand within the court of heaven,
Where white-robed pilgrims pass before my sight;
Earth's martyred saints and blood-washed overcomers,
These then are they who walk with Him in white.

When He shall call from earth's remotest corners
All who have stood triumphant in His might;
O to be worthy then to stand beside them,
And in that morn to walk with Him in white.

Almeda J. Pearce

His companions! "[Buy of me] white garments."

What is this talking about? If the gold speaks of the currency of heaven, and if the eye salve speaks of vision concerning things eternal, then the white garments speak to us of character, namely, of what we are. Oh, our lack of character, our secret sins! There cannot be a gathering of Christians as large as this without some leaders, respected leaders, who are guilty of secret sins.

It has been a sad privilege in some respects to have the place of leadership God has given me. But I've learned some things. Oh, how the Spirit of God has been grieved and how revival has been kept back because Christian leaders love their sins more than they love the Savior.

Is God talking to you about it? What about this business of buying white garments, the righteous acts of the saints? And these respectable sins of complacency, of dependency on devices, of the primacy of the secondary, the substitution of vehemency in defense of the faith for vitality in living the faith, superficiality—we're all right as long as we speak the language. God help us! Then there are the fleshly sins in thought, life, and action. And the sins of the spirit—bitterness, malice, envy, jealousy, pride, covetousness. God help us! "I counsel thee to buy of me white garments to cover thy nakedness."

What is the word God gives? You will find it in the same epistle, Revelation 3:19: "Repent," a word that we've forgotten, a word that we don't know much about, we don't know how to do it. But if we let God speak deeply enough to our souls, so that we see the heinousness of our sins and the emptiness of our professions, we'll be bowed down before Him and we'll be repenting even though we don't know the mechanics. God help us to get there.

Brother preacher and sister Christian worker, God is waiting for us. I'm not speaking absolutely against gadgets and devices and ideas and plans and promotion. They're all right in their places, but they are no substitute for sacrifice, for character, and for vision. Spirituality and discipline and discipleship and consecration and obedience are the need of this hour. We must get back to preaching the Word of God and to wrestling in prayer and to giving the artless, utterly honest witness of the Lord that is done in a forthright testimony for Him. We need to get back to first things.

Repent! And isn't it wonderful, "Behold, I stand at the door and knock" (Rev. 3:20). He is knocking tonight, and if you will open He will come in and He will sup with you as well as you will sup with Him.

I've tried to talk to you about something that God has been talking to me about, the Lord's counsel for us of the church of the present day. Will you let Him talk to you?

NOTES

A Pure Church An Increasing Church

Alexander Maclaren (1826–1910) was one of Great Britain's most famous preachers. While pastoring the Union Chapel, Manchester (1858–1903), he became known as "the prince of expository preachers." Rarely active in denominational or civic affairs, Maclaren invested his time in studying the Word in the original languages and sharing its truths with others in sermons that are still models of effective expository preaching. He published a number of books of sermons and climaxed his ministry by publishing his monumental *Expositions of Holy Scripture*.

This message was taken from *Christ the Heart,* published by Funk and Wagnalls in 1902.

Alexander Maclaren

4

A PURE CHURCH, AN INCREASING CHURCH

> And the Lord added to the church daily such as should be saved (Acts 2:47).
>
> And the Lord added to their number day by day those who were being saved (RSV).

YOU OBSERVE THAT the principal alterations in the Revised Standard Version of these words are two: the one the omission of "the church," the other the substitution of "were being saved" for "such as should be saved." The former of these changes has an interest as suggesting that, at the early period referred to, the name of "the church" had not yet been definitely attached to the infant community and that the word afterward crept into the text at a time when ecclesiasticism had become a great deal stronger than it was at the date of the writing of the Acts of the Apostles.

The second of the changes is of more importance. The Authorized Version's rendering suggests that salvation is a future thing, which in one aspect is partially true. The Revised Standard Version suggests the other idea, that salvation is a process going on all through the course of a Christian's life. And that carries very large and important lessons.

The Present Action of the Ascended Christ

I ask you to notice here, first, the profound conception that the writer had of the present action of the ascended Christ. "The Lord added to their number day by day those who were being saved."

Then, Christ (for it is He that is here spoken of as the Lord)—the living, ascended Christ—was present in, and working with, that little community of believing souls.

And you will find that the thought of a present Savior, who is the lifeblood of the church on earth and the spring of action for all good that is done in it and by it, runs through the whole of this book of the Acts of the Apostles.

The keynote of it is struck in its first verses: "The former treatise have I made, O Theophilus, of all that Jesus began both to do and teach, until the day in which he was taken up" (Acts 1:1–2). That is the description of Luke's gospel, and it implies that the Acts of the Apostles is the second treatise, which tells all that Jesus continued to do and teach after He was taken up. So the Lord, the ascended Christ, is the true theme and hero of this book. It is He, for instance, that sends down the Spirit on the Day of Pentecost. It is He whom the dying martyr sees "standing on the right hand of God" (7:55–56), ready to help. It is He who appears to the persecutor on the road to Damascus. It is He who sends Paul and his company to preach in Europe. It is He who opens hearts for the reception of their message. It is He who stands by the apostle in a vision and bids him be of good cheer and go forth upon his work. Thus, at every crisis in the history of the church, it is the Lord—that is to say, Christ Himself—who is revealed as working in them and for them, the ascended yet ever-present Guide, Counselor, Inspirer, Protector, and Rewarder of those that put their trust in Him. So here it is He who adds to the church daily those who were being saved.

I believe that modern Christianity has far too much lost the vivid impression of this present Christ as actually dwelling and working among us. What is good in us and what is bad in us conspire to make us think more of the past work of an ascended Christ than of the present work of an indwelling Christ. We cannot think too much of that Cross by which He has laid the foundation for the salvation and reconciliation of all the world. But we may easily think too exclusively of it and so fix our thoughts upon that work He completed when on Calvary He said, "It is finished!" (John 19:30) as to forget the continual work that will never be finished until His church is perfected and the world is redeemed. If we are a church of

Christ at all, we have Christ in very deed among us, working through us and on us. And unless we have, in no mystical and unreal and metaphorical sense but in the simplest and yet grandest prose reality, that living Savior here in our hearts and in our fellowship, better that these walls were leveled with the ground and this congregation scattered to the four winds of heaven. The present Christ is the life of His church.

Notice—and that but for a moment, for I shall have to deal with it more especially in another part of this discourse—the specific action that is here ascribed to Him. *He* adds to the church, not *we,* not our preaching, not our eloquence, not our fervor, not our efforts. These may be the weapons in His hands, but the hand that wields the weapon gives it all its power to wound and to heal. It is Christ Himself who, by His present energy, is here represented as being the agent of all the good that is done by any Christian community, and the builder up of these churches of His in numbers and in power.

It is His will, His ideal of a Christian church, that continuously it should be gathering into its fellowship those that are being saved. That is His meaning in the establishment of His church upon earth, and that is His will concerning it and concerning us. And the question should press on every society of Christians. Does our reality correspond to Christ's ideal? Are we, as a portion of His great heritage, being continually replenished by souls that come to tell what God has done for them? Is there an unbroken flow of such into what we call our communion? I speak to you members of this church, and I ask you to ponder the question—Is it so? I also ask you to ponder the other question—If it is not so, wherefore? "The Lord added . . . daily." Why does not the Lord add daily to us?

The Attractive Power of an Earnest and Pure Church

Let us go to the second part of this text and see if we can find an answer. Notice how emphatically there is brought out here the attractive power of an earnest and pure church.

My text is the end of a sentence. What is the beginning of the sentence? Listen! "All that believed were together, and had all things common; and sold their possessions and goods, and parted them to all men, as every man had need. And they, continuing daily with one accord in the temple, and breaking bread from house to house, did eat their meat with gladness and singleness of heart, praising God, and having favour with all the people. And the Lord added" (Acts 2:44–47). Yes! Of course. Suppose you were like these people. Suppose this church and congregation bore stamped upon it, plain and deep as the broad arrow of the king, these characteristics: manifest fraternal unity; plain unselfish unworldliness; habitual unbroken devotion; gladness, which had in it the solemnity of heaven; and a transparent simplicity of life and heart, which knew nothing of by-ends and shabby, personal motives or distracting duplicity of purpose. Do you not think that the Lord would add to you daily such as should be saved? Or, to put it into other words, wherever there is a little knot of men obviously held together by a living Christ and obviously manifesting in their lives and characters the features of that Christ transforming and glorifying them, there will be drawn to them—by natural gravitation, I was going to say, but we may more correctly say, by the gravitation that is natural in the supernatural realm—souls that have been touched by the grace of the Lord and souls to whom that grace has been brought the nearer by looking upon *them*. Wheresoever there is inward vigor of life there will be outward growth. The church that is pure, earnest, living will be a church that spreads and increases.

Historically, it has always been the case that in God's church seasons of expansion have followed upon seasons of deepened spiritual life on the part of His people. And the only kind of growth that is wholesome and to be desired in a Christian community is the growth as a consequence of the revived religiousness of the individuals who make up the community.

And just in like manner as such a community will draw to it men who are likeminded, so it will repel from it all the formalist people. There are congregations that have received the stamp of worldliness so deep upon them that the men who want to be burdened with as little religion as may be respectable will find themselves at home there. And I come to you Christian people here, for whose Christian character I am in some sense and to some degree responsible, with this appeal: Do you see to it that, so far as your influence extends, this community of ours be such as that half-dead Christians will never think of coming near us, and those whose religion is tepid will be repelled from us; but they who love the Lord Jesus Christ with earnest devotion and lofty consecration and seek to live unworldly and saintlike lives shall recognize in us people who are likeminded and from whom they may draw help. I beseech you—if you will not misunderstand the expression—make your communion such that it shall repel as well as attract; that people will find nothing here to draw them to an easy religion of words and formalism, beneath which all vermin of worldliness and selfishness may lurk, but shall recognize in us a church of men and women who are bent upon holiness, longing for more and more conformity to the Divine Master.

Now, if all this be true, it is possible for worldly and stagnant communities calling themselves churches to thwart Christ's purpose and to make it both impossible and undesirable that He should add to them the souls that He cares about. It is a solemn thing to feel that we may clog Christ's chariot wheels, that there may be so little spiritual life in us, as a congregation, that, if I may say so, He dare not entrust us with the responsibility of guarding and keeping the young converts whom He loves and tends. We may not be fit to be trusted with them, and that may be why we do not get them. It may not be good for them that they should be dropped into the refrigerating atmosphere of such a church, and that may be why they do not come.

Depend upon it, friends, that, far more than my preaching, your lives will determine the expansion of this church of ours. And if my preaching is pulling one way and your lives the other, and I have half an hour a week for talk and you have seven days for contradictory life, which of the two do you think is likely to win in the tug? I beseech you, take to yourselves the words that I am now trying to speak. Do not pass them to the man in the next pew and think how well they fit him, but accept them as needed by you. And remember that just as a bit of sealing wax, if you rub it on your sleeve and so warm it, develops an attractive power, the church that is warmed will draw many to itself. If the earlier words of this context apply to any Christian community, then certainly its blessed promise will apply to it too, and to such a church the Lord will add day by day those that are being saved.

The Class of Persons Gathered into the Community

And now, lastly, observe the definition given here of the class of persons gathered into the community.

I have already observed, in the earlier portions of this discourse, that here we have salvation represented as a process, a progressive thing that runs on all through life. In the New Testament there are various points of view from which that great idea of salvation is represented. It is sometimes spoken of as past, insofar as in the definite act of conversion and the first exercise of faith in Jesus Christ the whole subsequent evolution and development are involved, and the process of salvation has its beginning then when a man turns to God. It is sometimes spoken of as present, insofar as the joy of deliverance from evil and possession of good, which is God, is realized day by day. It is sometimes spoken of as future, insofar as all the imperfect possession and prelibations of salvation that we taste here on earth prophesy and point onward to their own perfecting in the climax of heaven. But all these three points of view—past, present, and future—may be merged into this one of my text, which speaks of every saint on earth, from the infantile to the most mature, as standing in the same row, though at different points; walking on the same road, though advanced different distances; all participant of the same process of "being saved."

Through all life the deliverance goes on, the deliverance from sin, the deliverance from wrath. The Christian salvation, then, according to the teaching of this emphatic phrase, is a process begun at conversion, carried on progressively through the life, and reaching its climax in another state. Day by day, through the spring and the early summer, the sun is longer in the sky and rises higher in the heavens. And the path of the Christian is as the shining light. Last year's greenwood is this year's hardwood, and the Christian, in like manner, has to grow in the grace and knowledge of the Lord and Savior. So these progressively and, therefore, as yet imperfectly saved people were gathered into the church.

Now I have but two things to say about that. If that be the description of the kind of folk that come into a Christian church, the duties of that church are very plainly marked. And the first great one is to see to it that the community help the growth of its members. There are Christian churches—I do not say whether ours is one of them or not—into which, if a young plant is brought, it is pretty sure to be killed. The temperature is so low that the tender shoots are burned as with frost and die. I have seen people coming all full of fervor and of faith into Christian congregations, and finding that the average around them was so much lower than their own, they have cooled down after a bit to the fashionable temperature and grown indifferent like their fellow Christians. Let us, dear friends, remember that a Christian church is a nursery of imperfect Christians and, for ourselves and for one another, try to make our communion such as shall help shy and tender graces to unfold themselves and woo out by the encouragement of example the lowest and the least perfect to lofty holiness and consecration like the Master's.

And if I am speaking to any in this congregation who hold aloof from Christian fellowship for more or less sufficient reasons, let me press upon them, in one word, that if they are conscious of however imperfect a possession of that incipient salvation, their place is thereby determined and they are doing wrong if they do not connect themselves with some Christian communion and stand forth as members of Christ's church.

And now one last word. I have tried to show you that salvation, in the New Testament, is regarded as a process. The opposite thing is a process too. There is a very awful contrast in one of Paul's epistles. "The word of the cross is folly to those *who are perishing,* but to us who are *being saved* it is the power of God" (1 Cor. 1:18 RSV, emphasis added). These two processes start, as it were, from the same point, one by slow degrees and almost imperceptible motion, rising higher and higher; the other by slow degrees and almost unconscious descent, sliding steadily and fatally downward ever further and further.

And my point now is that in each of us one or other of these processes is going on. Either you are slowly rising or you are slipping down. Either a larger measure of the life of Christ, which is salvation, is passing into your hearts, or bit by bit you are dying as some man with creeping paralysis that begins at the extremities and with fell, silent, inexorable footstep advances further and further toward the citadel of the heart, where it lays its icy hand at last, and the man is dead. You are either being saved or you are perishing. No man becomes a devil all at once, and no man becomes an angel all at once. Trust yourself to Christ and He will lift you to Himself; turn your back upon Him, as some of you are doing, and you will settle down, down, down in the muck and the mire of your own sensuality and selfishness, until at last the foul ooze spreads over your head, and you are lost in the bog forever.

NOTES

The Ministry of a Transfigured Church

John Henry Jowett (1864–1923) was known as "the greatest preacher in the English-speaking world." He was born in Yorkshire, England. He was ordained into the Congregational ministry, and his second pastorate was at the famous Carr's Lane Church, Birmingham, where he followed the eminent Dr. Robert W. Dale. From 1911 to 1918, he pastored the Fifth Avenue Presbyterian Church, New York City; from 1918 to 1923, he ministered at Westminster Chapel, London, succeeding G. Campbell Morgan. He wrote many books of devotional messages and sermons.

This message was taken from *Great Pulpit Masters,* volume 5, published by Fleming H. Revell in 1950.

John Henry Jowett

5

THE MINISTRY OF A TRANSFIGURED CHURCH

And when the day of Pentecost was now come, they were all together in one place. And suddenly there came from heaven a sound as of a rushing mighty wind, and it filled all the house where they were sitting. And there appeared unto them tongues parting asunder, like as of fire; and it sat upon each one of them. And they were all filled with the Holy Spirit, and began to speak with other tongues, as the Spirit gave them utterance.

. . . And when this sound was heard, the multitude came together (Acts 2:1–4, 6 ASV).

THE WONDER INSIDE the church aroused inquisitive interest without. There came to the church an exceptional and plentiful endowment, and, as by the constraint of a mystic gravitation, the outside crowd began to move like the waters swayed by the moon. The crowd may have moved toward the church in the temper of a flippant curiosity or in the spirit of unfriendly revolt or in the solemn mood of appropriating awe. Whatever may have been the constraint, the waters were no longer stagnant, the masses were no longer heedless and apathetic. The heedlessness was broken up, interest was begotten, and "the multitude came together."

Is the modern church the center of similar interest and wonder? Is there any awed and mesmeric rumor breathing through the streets, stirring the indifferent heart into eager questions? The modern church claims immediate kinship and direct and vital lineage with that primitive fellowship in the Upper Room. Does she manifest the power of the early church? Does she reveal the same magnetic influence and constraint?

I know that "the kingdom of God cometh not with observation" (Luke 17:20). And so it is with the spring. The spring "cometh not with observation," but you speedily have tokens that she is here. She can hide her coming behind March squalls, and she can step upon our shores in the rough attire of a blustering and tempestuous day. But even though her coming may be without observation, her presence cannot be hid. And even so it is with the kingdom: she may make no noisy and ostentatious display of her coming, but the sleeping seeds feel her approach, the valley of bones experiences an awakening thrill, and "there is nothing hid from the heat thereof" (Ps. 19:6). I think, therefore, that we are justified in seriously inquiring as to the resurrection power of our churches, the measure of their quickening influence, their net result in reaching and stirring and consecrating the energies of a community. How do they stand in the judgment? Is the Pentecostal morning repeated, and is the gracious miracle the talk of the town? Does the multitude come together, greatly wondering?

Carry the inquisition to the regular and frequent fellowship of the church. So many times a week her members gather together in the Upper Room. What happens in the hallowed shrine? Are we held in solemn and enriching amazement at the awful doings? And when we come forth again, is there about us a mysterious impressiveness that arrests the multitude and that sends abroad a spirit of questioning like a healthy contagion? Can we honestly say that by our ordinary services the feet of the heedless crowd are stayed and that the people come together greatly wondering? In answer to all these searching questions I think that even the most optimistic of us will feel obliged to confess that the general tendency is undisturbed, that we do not generate force enough to stop the drift, and that the surrounding multitude remains uninfluenced.

Now, when we consider these unattracted or alienated peoples, we can roughly divide them into three primary classes. First, there are those who never think about us at all. So very remote are the highways of their thought and life that the impulse of the church is spent before it reaches their mental and moral abode. We can scarcely describe their attitude as one of indifference because the mood of indifference would imply a negligent sense of our existence, and I can discern no signs of such perception. We contribute no thread to the warp and woof of their daily lives. We bring no nutriment to the common meal. We do not even provide a condiment for the feast. Our presence in the city brings neither pleasure nor pain, neither sweet nor bitter, neither irritation nor ease. Their souls are not disquieted within them, neither are they lulled into a deeper and more perilous sleep. We are neither irritants nor sedatives. To this particular class we simply do not exist.

And then, secondly, there are those who have thought about us and as a result of their thinking have determined to ignore us. For all simple, positive, and progressive purposes we are no longer any good. We are exhausted batteries. We have no longer the power to ring a loud alarm or to light a new road or to energize some heavy and burdensome crusade. Our once stern and sacrificial warfare has now become a bloodless and self-indulgent quest. It is not only that the once potent shell cases have been emptied of their explosive content, they have been converted into dinner gongs! The once brilliant and unconditional ethical ideal has been dimmed and shadowed by worldly compromise. The pure and oxygenated flame of righteous passion has been changed into the fierce but smoky bonfire of sectarian zeal. We are looked upon as engaged in petty and childish controversy, losing ourselves in vague and nebulous phraseology, decking ourselves in vestures and postures as harmless and indifferent as the dresses worn at a fancy ball. That is the estimate formed of us by a vast section of the thinking crowd. You will find it reflected week by week in the labor papers where we are regarded as straws in some side bay of a mighty river, riding serenely round and round and round. We do not even show the drift of the stream, the dominant movement of our age. Our speech and our doings are of interest to the antiquary, but for all serious, practical, forceful, and aspiring life our churches do not count.

And, thirdly, there are those who think about us and who are constrained by their thinking into the fiercest and most determined opposition. To these men the church is not like Bunyan's "Giant Pope," alive but impotent, and "by reason of age, and also of the many shrewd brushes that he met with in his younger days, grown so crazy and stiff in his joints that he can do little more than sit in his cave's mouth, grinning at pilgrims as they go by, and biting his nails because he cannot come at them." No, to this class the church can do more than grin, it can reach and tear; its ministry is still destructive. Its influence is perverse and perverting. Its very faith is a minister of mental and moral paralysis. Its dominant conceptions befog the common atmosphere and chill and freeze "the genial currents of the soul." Its common postures and practices, its defenses and aggressions, perpetuate and confirm human alienations and divisions. The church cannot be ignored. It is not a harmless and picturesque ruin. It is a foul fungus souring the common soil, and for the sake of all sweet and beautiful things, its nefarious influence must be destroyed.

This is by no means an exhaustive analysis of the alienated multitude, but it is sufficiently descriptive for my present purpose. In each of these three great primary classes the people stand aloof, indifferent, and resentful. The church is not endowed with that subduing and triumphant impressiveness that would turn their reverent feet toward herself. Now, how stands it with the church? Does she seem fitted to strike and arrest and silence and allure the careless or suspicious multitudes? What is there unique and amazing about her? Her Lord has promised her a marvelous distinctiveness. She is to be "a glorious church, not having spot, or wrinkle, or any such thing" (Eph. 5:27).

"A glorious church," shining amid all the surrounding twilights with the radiance of a splendid noon! "Not having spot": no defect, no blemish, no impaired function, no diseased limb! "Or wrinkle": there shall be no sign of age about her or any waste. She shall never become an anachronism. She shall always be as young as the present age, ever distinguished by her youthful brow and by her fresh and almost boisterous optimism! "Or wrinkle, or any such thing." Mark the final, holy swagger of it, as though by a contemptuous wave of the hand the apostle indicates the entire rout of the unclean pests that invade and attack an apostate church. "Or any such thing"! Are these great words of promise in any high degree descriptive of our own church? Is this our distinctiveness? "Not having spot": have we no withered hands, no halt, no blind, no lame, no lepers? "Or wrinkle": are we really distinguished by the invincible and contagious energies of perpetual youth? Does not the holding up of this great ideal throw our basal defects into dark and ugly relief?

The pity of it all is just this, that the church, with all its loud and exuberant professions, is exceedingly like "the world." There is no clean, clear line of separation. In place of the promised glories, we have a tolerable and unexciting dimness; in place of superlative whiteness, we have an uninteresting gray; in place of the spirit of an aggressive youthfulness, we have a loitering and time-serving expediency. There would be no difficulty—if only we had seized upon the fullness of our resources and had become clothed with the riches of our promised inheritance—in men being able to distinguish, in any general company, the representatives of the church of the living God. There would be about them the pervasive joy of spiritual emancipation, resting upon all their speech and doings like sunlight on the hills. There would be about them a spiritual spring and buoyance, which would enable them to move amid besetting obstacles with the nimbleness of a hart. "He maketh my feet like hinds' feet" (2 Sam. 22:34; Ps. 18:33)! "By my God have I leaped over a wall" (2 Sam. 22:30; Ps. 18:29)! There would be about them the fine serenity that is born of a mighty alliance. And there would be the strong, healthy pulse of a holy and hallowing purpose, beating in constant and forceful persistence. Such characteristics would distinguish any man and any company and any church, and the startled multitude would gather around in questioning curiosity.

But the alluring wonder is largely absent from our church. Men pass from the world into our precincts as insensible of any difference as though they had passed from one side of the street to the other, not feeling as though they had been transported from the hard, sterile glare of the city thoroughfare into the fascinating beauties of the Devonshire lane.

What, then, do we need? We need the return of the wonder, the arresting marvel of a transformed church, the phenomenon of a miraculous life. I speak not now of the wonders of spasmodic revivals. Indeed, if I must be perfectly frank, my confidence in the efficient ministry of these elaborately engineered revivals has greatly waned. I will content myself with the expression of this most sober judgment that the alienated and careless multitude is not impressed by the machinery and products of our modern revivals. The ordinary mission does not, and cannot, reach the stage at which this particular type of impressiveness becomes operative. The impressiveness does not attach to "decisions," but to resultant life. The wonder of the world is not excited by the phenomena of the penitent bench but by what happens at the ordinary workbench in the subsequent days. The world is not impressed by the calendar statement that at a precise particular moment winter relinquished her sovereignty to spring. The real interest is awakened by the irresistible tokens of the transition in garden, hedgerow, and field. It is not the new birth that initially arrests the world but the new and glorified life. It is not, therefore, by spasmodic revivals, however grace-blessed they may be, that we shall excite the wonder of the multitude but by the abiding miracle of a God-filled and glorious church.

What we need, above all things, is the continuous marvel of an elevated church, "set on high" by the King, having her home "in the heavenly place is Christ," approaching all things "from above," and triumphantly resisting the subtle gravitation of "the world, the flesh, and the devil." It is not only multitudes of decisions that we want, but preeminently the heightening of the life of the saved, the glorification of the saints. The great

Evangelical Revival began not with the reclamation of the depraved but with the enrichment of the redeemed. It was the members of the Holy Club, moving amid the solemnities of grace and sacred fellowship, who were lifted up into the superlative stages of the spiritual life and who in that transition took a step as great and vital as the earlier step from sin to righteousness. Their life became a high and permanent miracle, and their subsequent ministry was miraculous. That is the most urgent necessity of our day, a church of the superlative order, immeasurably heightened and enriched—a church with wings as well as feet, her dimness changed into radiance, her stammering changed into boldness, and presenting to the world the spectacle of a permanent marvel, which will fascinate and allure the inquiring multitude—drawn together not that they might see Jesus only, but "Lazarus also, whom he had raised from the dead" (John 12:9).

Now, what is the explanation of the comparative poverty and impotence of our corporate life? Why is the church not ladened with the impressive dignities of her destined inheritance? Look at the manner of our fellowship. Is it such as to give promise of power and wealth? When we meet together, in worshiping communities, do we look like men and women who are preparing to move amid the amazing and enriching sanctities of the Almighty? Take our very mode of entry. It is possible to lose a thing by the way we approach it. I have seen a body of flippant tourists on the Rigi at the dawn, and by their noisy irreverence they missed the very glory they had come to see. "When ye come to appear before me, who hath required this at your hand, to trample my courts?" (Isa. 1:12 ASV). That loud and irreverent tramp is far too obtrusive in our communion. We are not sufficiently possessed by that spirit of reverence which is the open sesame into the realms of light and grace. We are not subdued into the receptiveness of awe. No, it is frequently asserted that in our day awe is an undesirable temper, a relic of an obsolete stage, a remnant of pagan darkness, a fearful bird of a past night, altogether a belated anachronism in the full, sweet light of the evangel of grace.

I remember receiving a firm, but very courteous, letter of remonstrance from one of the children of light because on the very threshold of a lovely summer's morning I had announced the hymn:

Lo! God is here: let us adore
And own how dreadful is this place.

And my friend said it was like going back to the cold, gray dawn, when disturbed spirits were speeding to their rest! It was like moving amid the shadows and specters of Genesis, and he wanted to lie and bask in the calm, sunny noon of the Gospel by John! I think his letter was representative of a common and familiar mood of our time. I have no desire to return to the chill, uncertain hours of the early morning, but I am concerned that we should learn and acquire the only receptive attitude in the presence of our glorious noon. It is certain that many of the popular hymns of our day are very far removed from the hymn to which I have just referred. It is not that these hymns are essentially false but that they are so one-sided as to throw the truth into disproportion, and so they impair and impoverish the spiritual life.

Here is one of the more popular hymns of our time:

O that will be glory for me,
When by His grace I shall look on His face,
That will be glory for me!

Well, we all want to share in the inspiration of the great expectancy! It is a light and lifting song with very nimble feet, but lest our thought should fashion itself after the style of these tripping strains, we need to hear behind the lilt "the voice of the great Eternal," sobering our very exuberance into deep and awful joy. "When by His grace I shall look on His face!" That is one aspect of the great outlook, and only one, and therefore incomplete. I find the complementary aspect in these familiar words, "With twain he covered his face!" That is quite another outlook, and it introduces the deepening ministry of awe, which I am afraid is so foreign to the modern mind. "I feel like singing all the day!" So runs another of our popular hymns. That would have been a congenial song for my friend on that radiant summer morning when his thoughtless minister led him up to the awful splendors of the Great White Throne! "I feel like singing all the day," and the words suggest that this ought to be the normal mood for all pilgrims on the heavenly way. I am not so sure about that, and I certainly have grave doubts as to whether the man who feels like singing all the day will make the best soldier when it comes to "marching as to war." "The LORD is in his holy temple: let all the earth keep silence before him" (Hab. 2:20). That is a contemplation which seeks expression in something deeper than song. "There was silence in heaven about the space of half an hour" (Rev. 8:1). What had they seen, what had they heard, what further visions of glory had been unveiled that speech and song were hushed, and the soul sought fitting refuge in an awe-inspired silence?

When I listen to our loud and irreverent tramp, when I listen to so many of our aweless hymns and prayers, I cannot but ask whether we have lost those elements from our contemplation that are fitted to subdue the soul into silence and to deprive it of the clumsy expedient of speech. We leave our places of worship, and no deep and inexpressible wonder sits upon our faces. We can sing these lifting melodies, and when we go out into the streets our faces are one with the faces of those who have left the theaters and the music halls. There is nothing about us to suggest that we have been looking at anything stupendous and overwhelming. Far back in my boyhood I remember an old saint telling me that after some services he liked to make his way home alone by quiet byways, so that the hush of the Almighty might remain on his awed and prostrate soul. That is the element we are losing, and its loss is one of the measures of our poverty, and the primary secret of our inefficient lives and service.

And what is the explanation of the loss? Preeminently our impoverished conception of God. The popular God is not great and will not create a great race. The church must not expect to strike humanity with startling and persistent impact if she carries in her own mind and heart the enfeebling image of a mean Divinity. Men who are possessed by a powerful God can never themselves be impotent. But have we not robbed the Almighty of much of His awful glory, and to that extent are we not ourselves despoiled? We have contemplated the beauties of the rainbow, but we have overlooked the dim severities of the throne. We have toyed with the light, but we have forgotten the lightning. We have rejoiced in the fatherhood of our God, but too frequently the fatherhood we have proclaimed has been throneless and effeminate. We have picked and chosen according to the weakness of our own tastes and not according to the full-orbed revelation of the truth. We have selected the picturesque and rejected the appalling. "And he had in his right hand seven stars"—yes, we can accept that delicate suggestion of encircling love and care! "And his countenance was as the sun shineth in his strength"—yes, we can bask in the distributed splendor of the sunny morn! "And out of his mouth went a sharp twoedged sword!" (Rev. 1:16)—and is that too in our selection, or has our cherished image been deprived of the sword? Why leave out that sword? Does its absence make us more thoughtful and braver men, or does it tend to lull us into an easefulness that removes us far away from the man who when he saw Him, "fell at his feet as dead" (v. 17)?

This mild, enervating air of our modern Lutheranism needs to be impregnated with something of the bracing salts of Calvinism. Our very evangelicalism would be all the sturdier by the addition of a little "baptized Stoicism." Our water has become too soft, and it will no longer make bone for a race of giants. Our Lutheranism has been diluted and weakened by the expulsion of some of the sterner motive-elements that it possessed at its source. If we banish the conceptions that inspire awe, we of necessity devitalize the very doctrines of grace. If grace is emasculated, then faith becomes anemic, and we take away the very tang and pang from the sense of sin. All the great epistles of the apostle Paul being in the awe-inspiring heights of towering mountain country, and all through the changing applications of the thought, these cloud-capped eminences are ever in sight. Paul's eyes were always lifted up unto the hills, and therefore his soul was always on its knees. If he rejoiced, it was "with trembling"; if he served the Lord, it was "with fear"; if he was "perfecting holiness," it was gain "in the fear of the Lord!" Always, I say, this man's eyes were upon the awful, humbling, and yet inspiring heights of revealed truth.

Our modern theological country is too flat; there are not enough cool, uplifted snow-white heights—heights like Lebanon—to which the peasant can turn his feverish eyes even when he is engaged in the labors of the sweltering vale. "Will a man leave the snow of Lebanon?" (Jer. 18:14). "Thy righteousness is like the great mountains" (Ps. 36:6)! "Go . . . stand upon the mount before the LORD" (1 Kings 19:11). "In the year that king Uzziah died I saw also the Lord . . . high and lifted up. . . . Holy, holy, holy, is the LORD" (Isa. 6:1, 3). That was a mountain view. "Then said I, Woe is me!" (v. 5). And that was the consequent awe. If the ministers of the church were to dwell in those vast uplifted solitudes, strange things would happen to us. Our speech would be deepened in content and tone, and we should speak as they say John Fletcher of Madeley used to speak, "Like one who had just left the immediate converse of God and angels." But not only so, there would be added to our speech the awful energy of a still more powerful silence. "Every year makes me tremble," said Bishop Westcott toward the end of his years, "every year makes me tremble at the daring with which people speak of spiritual things." Is not the good bishop's trembling justified?

Some time ago I preached a sermon on the bitter cup that was drunk by our Lord and Savior Jesus Christ. I noticed that one of the papers, in a reference to the sermon, said that I had spoken on the sufferings of Christ "with charming effect." The words sent me to my knees in humiliation and fear. Soul of mine, what had I said, or what had I left unsaid, or through what perverting medium had I been interpreted? For the flippancy can be in the reporter as well as in the preacher; it can be in the religious press as well as in the consecrated minister. But let the application stand to me alone and let me once again remind myself of Westcott's trembling "at the daring with which people speak of spiritual things." Aye, we are reckless and therefore forceless in our speech; we are not mighty in our silences. There are some things that our people must infer from our reverent silences, things that can never be told in speech, and these mountain experiences are among them. That awe of the heights will deepen and enlarge both the ministry and the church, it will enrich both her speech and her silences, and it will make her character unspeakably masculine, forceful, and impressive.

"If in any part of Europe a man was required to be burned, or broken on the wheel, that man was at Geneva, ready to depart, giving thanks to God, and singing psalms to Him." A mighty God makes irresistible men. History has proved, and experience confirms it today, that this mountain thinking, with all its subduing austerities and shadows, would create a powerful and athletic church, a church of most masculine temper, courageous both in its aggressions and in its restraints, both in its confessions and its reserves, a church that would rouse and impress the world by the decisive vigor of its daily life—never dull, never feeble, but always and everywhere "fair as the moon, clear as the sun, and terrible as an army with banners" (Song 6:10). "O Zion . . . get thee up into the high mountain" (Isa. 40:9).

But our impoverished conception of God is not the only cause of our comparative poverty and enfeeblement. The life of the church is expressed in two relationships, the human and the Divine. The Divine fellowship has been impoverished by lack of height; the human fellowship has been impoverished by lack of breadth. We have not drunk the iron water from the heart of the mountains, and we have therefore lacked a healthy robustness. We have not accumulated the manifold treasures of the far-stretching plain, and we have therefore lacked a wealthy variety. Our fellowship with God has been mean; our fellowship with man has been scanty. No, would it not be just the truth to say that the human aspects of our church fellowship suggest a treasure-house that has never been unlocked?

The church is poor because much of her treasure is imprisoned, but she herself carries the liberating key to the iron gate! Our riches are buried in the isolated lives of individual members instead of all being pooled for the endowment of the whole fraternity. A very large part of the ample ministry of the χοινωνία has been atrophied, if indeed it has ever been well sustained. I gratefully recognize the mystic, silent fellowship among the consecrated members of the church of Christ. I know that out of the very heart of "[him] that believeth" there inevitably "flow rivers of living water" (John 7:38), and I delight to allow my imagination to rest upon the well-irrigated country of this sanctified society. There is a mystic commerce altogether independent of human expedient or arrangement. We cannot bow together without some exchange of heavenly merchandise, without angel ministries carrying from island to island the unique and peculiar products of their climes. The rich and enriching history of the Society of Friends is altogether corroborative of this great truth of spiritual experience. "When I came into the silent assemblies of God's people," says Robert Barclay, "I felt a sweet power among them which touched my heart, and as I gave way unto it, I found the evil weakening in me and the good raised up."

But the human side of the apostolic χοινωνία includes riches other than these. It is not only a mystic interchange in the awful depths of the spirit; it is a fellowship of intelligence, it is a community of experience, it is the socializing of the individual testimony and witness. It is not only the subtle carriage of spiritual energy, it is the transference of visions, the sharing of discoveries, the assemblage of many judgments, whether in the hour of triumph or of defeat. "When ye come together, every one of you hath a psalm, hath a doctrine, hath a tongue, hath a revelation, hath an interpretation" (1 Cor. 14:26). That is the broader fellowship we lack, and we are all the poorer for it. The psalm that is born in one heart remains unsung, and the sadness it was fitted to remove from the heart of another abides like a clammy mist. The revelation that dawned upon one wondering soul is never shared, and so another remains in the cold imprisonment of the darkness. The private interpretation is never given, and for want of the key, many obstructing doors are never unlocked.

This is the neglected side of the apostolic fellowship, and for the want of it the church goes out to confront the world in the poverty of a starved individualism rather than in the rich and full-blooded vigor of her communistic strength. We are not realizing the social basis of the church's life. Christian fellowship comprehends not only a meeting at a common altar, but a meeting at a family hearth for the reverent and familiar interchange of our experiences with God and of what has happened to us in our warfare with the world, the flesh, and the Devil. In lieu of the broader and richer fellowship, we have exalted the ministry of one man, and out of the limited pool of his experience—and sometimes they are not even experiences but only fond and desirable assumptions—the whole community has to drink, while the rest of the many pools remain untapped. And, oh, the treasures that are hidden in these unshared and unrevealed experiences!

What have our matured saints to tell us of the things we wish to know? How did they escape the snare, or by what subtlety were they fatally beguiled? How did they take the hill, and where did they discover the springs of refreshing? What did they find to be the best footgear when the gradient was steep, and how did they comfort their hearts when they dug the grave by the way? What is it like to grow old? What delicacies does the Lord of the road provide for aged pilgrims, and have they seen any particular and wonderful stars in their evening sky? Are not all of us unspeakably poorer because these counsels and inspirations are untold? And our younger communicants—how are they faring on the new and arduous road? What unsuspected difficulties are they meeting? And what unsuspected provisions have they received?

And what privilege of service has been given them, and what inspiring vision have they found in the task? And what have our stalwart warriors to tell us? How goes the fight in the business fields, on market and exchange? And what hidden secret has the Lord of light been unveiling to the ordained layman? What wealth of truth and glory? I say, these are breadths of the χοινωνία we do not traverse, these are mines we do not work, and the output of our moral and spiritual energy is consequently small.

I know the perils that abound in these particular regions of exercised communion. Those who have the least to say may be readiest to speak. The spiritually insolvent may rise and talk like spiritual millionaires. The bloom of a delicate reserve may be destroyed, and flippant witnessing may become a substitute for deep experience. Easy familiarity may be made the standard of spiritual attainment, and sensational statements may be engendered by the hotbed of vanity and pride. In a fellowship meeting some members may speak from a subtle love of applause, while others may speak from an equally illicit sense of shame. I know all this, but I know also that there is nothing in the entire round of Christian worship and communion that is not exposed to abomination and abuse. There is not a single plant in your garden that is not the gathering ground of some particular pest; aye, and the more delicate and tender the plant, the more multitudinous are the foes. But you do not banish the plant because of the pests; you accept the plant and guard against the pests. I, for one, think it not impossible to cultivate this larger, richer, more social and familiar fellowship and at the same time to create an atmosphere in which these invasive perils shall be unable to breathe.

Under God, everything depends upon your leader. And under God, cannot wise leaders be grown-leaders who shall be able, with a rare delicacy of tact born of deep and unceasing communion with God, to draw out the individual gift of witness and experience, and by the accumulated treasure to enrich the entire church? Our church is comparatively poor and unimpressive. Here is a storehouse of untouched resources that I am convinced would immeasurably enrich and strengthen our equipment in our combined attack against the powers of darkness. We need to get higher up the mountains. And we need, also, to get farther out upon the plains. "O, for a closer walk with God!" And, "O, for a closer walk with man!" Closer to the great and holy God, that we may be possessed by a deepening and fertilizing awe; closer to our brother, that we may move in the manifold inspiration and comfort of mutual faith and experience.

I have not been concerned with the suggestion of new expedients. It has not been my purpose to advocate or defend aggressive and unfamiliar enterprises. My eyes have not been upon the church's conduct but upon her character; not upon her prospectus but upon her capital; not upon her plan of campaign but upon her fighting strength. "Like a mighty army moves the church of God!" Yes, but does she? Are not her regiments sometimes almost Falstaffian in their bedraggled impotence? How shall she increase her fighting power? How shall she enrich her spirit of discipline? And I have answered: By taking thought of the untrodden heights and the untrodden breadths within her own circle, by claiming her purposed and buried resources in humanity and in God. I am convinced that in these ways we should make undreamed of additions to the energy and impact of the church's strength. No church can walk along these unfrequented paths without acquiring the moments of sacrificial grace. When the power of the church becomes awful and sacrificial, when she bears in her body the red "marks of the Lord Jesus" (Gal. 6:17), when there is "blood upon the lintel, and on the two side posts" (Ex. 12:23) of her door, you may be assured that the arrested multitude will come together, drawn by the mesmeric gravitation of her own irresistible strength.

And not only strong shall the church become, strong in unselfish daring and persistence, but because of the very robustness of her strength she shall be tender with an exquisitely delicate compassion. I have yielded to none in the advocacy of the wooing note in the ministry of the Word, and with a growing and richer confidence I advocate it still. But there is the wooing note of a silly, simpering sentimentalism, and there is the wooing note of strong and masculine men who have been cradled and molded and taught in the austere nursery and school of the mountains. And where can you make your fine wooers if not among the deepening ministries of the mountains? "How beautiful upon the mountains are the feet of him that bringeth good tidings!" I shall have no fear about the strength and sweetness of the wooing note when we are all the children of the heights.

Given these conditions, I believe the church will move among the alienated multitudes with an illumined and fascinating constraint. The alienation of the people is not fundamental and ultimate. Deep down, beneath all the visible severances, there are living chords of kinship, ready to thrill and to respond to the royal note. Those living chords—buried, if you will, beneath the dead and deadening crust of formality and sin, buried, but buried alive—are to be found in Belgravia, where Henry Drummond, that man of the high mountains and the broad plains, awoke them to response by the strong, tender impact of a great evangel and a great experience. And those living chords are also to be found at the pit's mouth among the crooked and pathetic miners, and they become vibrant with responsive devotion, as Keir Hardie has told us that his became vibrant in answer to the awakening sweep of the strong, tender hands of the Nazarene. The multitude is not sick of Jesus; it is only sick of His feeble and bloodless representatives. When once again a great church appears, a church with the Lord's name in her forehead, a church with fine muscular limbs and face seamed with the marks of sacrifice, the multitude will turn their feet to the way of God's commandments.

I sat a little while ago in one of the chambers of the National Gallery, and my attention was caught by the vast miscellaneous crowd as it sauntered and galloped through the rooms. All sorts and conditions of people passed by—rich and poor, the well dressed and the beggarly, students and artisans, soldiers and sailors, maidens just out of school and women bowed and wrinkled in age. But, whoever they were, and however unarresting may have been all the other pictures in the chamber, every single soul in that mortal crowd stopped dead and silent before a picture of our Savior bearing His cross to the hill. And when the church is seen to be His body, His very body—His lips, His eyes, His ears, His hands, His feet, His brain, His heart, His very body—and when the church repeats, in this her corporate life, the brave and manifold doings of Judea and Galilee, she too shall awe the multitude. By God's grace she shall convert the meaningful wonder into deep and grateful devotion.

Our times are disturbed, and hopefully and fruitfully disturbed, by vast and stupendous problems. On every side the latch is lifting, and the door of opportunity stands ajar. But we shall fail in our day, as other men have failed in their day, unless by faith and experience we enter into "the fellowship of his sufferings," and become clothed with "the power of his resurrection" (Phil. 3:10). Sound social economics are not enough; sound political principles are not enough; sound creeds and politics are not enough. The most robust and muscular principle will faint and grow weary unless it is allied with character that is rendered unique and irresistible by unbroken communion with the mind and will of God. It is Christ in us that is "the hope of glory" (Col. 1:27), both for the individual and the state.

Let all of us abide in Him in total and glorious self-abandonment. Let nothing move us from our rootage. Let us pray without ceasing (1 Thess. 5:17), and let our consecration be so complete and confident that there may be presented to the world a church "alive unto God" (Rom. 6:11); a church as abounding in signs of vitality as hedgerows in the spring; a church quickened in moral vision, in intellectual perception, in emotional discernment. Let us present to the world a church acute, compassionate, and daring, moving amid the changing circumstances of men in the very spirit of her Lord and presenting everywhere the arresting ministry of "an hiding place from the wind, and a covert from the tempest; as rivers of water in a dry place, as the shadow of a great rock in a weary land" (Isa. 32:2).

The Church—Conservative and Aggressive

Charles Haddon Spurgeon (1834–1892) is undoubtedly the most famous minister of the nineteenth century. Converted in 1850, he united with the Baptists and soon began to preach in various places. He became pastor of the Baptist church in Waterbeach, England, in 1851, and three years later he was called to the decaying Park Street Church, London. Within a short time the work began to prosper, a new church was built and dedicated in 1861, and Spurgeon became London's most popular preacher. In 1855, he began to publish his sermons weekly; today they make up the fifty-seven volumes of *The Metropolitan Tabernacle Pulpit*. He founded a pastor's college and several orphanages.

This sermon was taken from *The Metropolitan Tabernacle Pulpit,* volume 7.

Charles Haddon Spurgeon

6

THE CHURCH—CONSERVATIVE AND AGGRESSIVE

> The church of the living God, the pillar and ground of the truth (1 Timothy 3:15).

YOU WILL REMEMBER it was announced last Sunday that a collection would be made today in behalf of our institution for training young men for the ministry. It has been thought desirable that I should state a few particulars relative to the institution. Some of them will appear in the course of the sermon.

It may suffice for me to say now that some five or six years ago one of the young men of the church gave promise of being a successful minister if he could but have a good education. With the assistance of a friend in the church, I undertook to take him under my charge, to put him under a suitable tutor, and to train him for the ministry. So successful was that work that I was induced to take another and another and another. Up to this time, I have been myself committee, secretary, treasurer, and subscriber. I have not, except in one or two instances, even mentioned the matter to anyone. I have been content to spare everything that I could out of my own income, besides that which is necessary for the support of my household, in order to educate any young men who came in my way that they might become ministers of the Cross of Christ.

There are now seven settled out, all of whom have been eminently successful. They are probably not men who will become great or brilliant, but they have been good and useful preachers. I think there are no other seven preachers in the whole Baptist denomination who have had so many converts during the years that they have been settled. They have been the means, most of them, in the hands of God of adding a very considerable number every year to the churches where they have settled, and those are churches not in provincial towns but in villages.

I have, therefore, been led still further to increase my number. I think I have now about sixteen young men wholly to support and maintain. Besides these, there is a very considerable number who receive their education in the evening, though they still remain in their own callings. With the enlarged sphere we now occupy as a church, I have proposed so to enlarge my scheme that all the members of this church and congregation who happen to be deficient in the plain rudiments of knowledge can get an education—a common English education for themselves. Then, if they display any ability for speaking, without giving up their daily avocations, they shall have classes provided for higher branches of instruction. But should they feel that God has called them to the ministry, I am then prepared, after the use of my own judgment and the judgment of my friends as to whether they are fit persons, to give them two years' special tutorship that they may go forth to the work of the Cross, thoroughly trained so far as we can effect it in so short a time.

I know I am called to this work, and I have had some most singular interpositions of providence in providing funds for it up until now. At the day of judgment the world shall know that there has never lived a man upon the face of the earth who has less deserved the calumny of seeking to enrich himself than I have. I shall say no more upon that. Let the world scandalize me if it will. I want the money today not for myself in any respect. I give my services and my work freely, and of my own income all that I can spare. I only want my friends who feel interested in this work to assist me, that we may provide men who shall preach the Gospel to multitudes who are longing to hear it fully and faithfully proclaimed.

Permit me to say there was held in Westminster Abbey last Thursday a grand choral festival at which there were singers from various choirs of London—St. Paul's, the

Abbey, the Temple, and the Foundling, and some from Windsor besides. Several ecclesiastical dignitaries graced the assembly. Anthems and cantatas, and I know not what else, were performed on a most classic scale. The sermon was preached by a provost of some college, in which the claims of the Society for the Propagation of the Gospel in Foreign Parts were eloquently advocated, and the whole collection amounted to seventy pounds. "A very poor result for so sublime a service," said the *Times* report.

Last Friday evening there was held a little meeting in one of the rooms here of about forty or fifty of the seat holders in this congregation. There were no bishops present. There were only a few street preachers and my poor students. They addressed that little meeting, and though no collection was called for or even contemplated, those friends spontaneously subscribed one hundred and eighty pounds as an earnest of what they were sure the congregation would give to this work today. I think this just shows that when people have a mind for Christ's cause, they do not need to have the state to support their religion but can support it out of the generosity of loving hearts without the elaborate parade of gorgeous rituals.

I shall now invite your attention to the subject of this morning's discourse, which has a very strong bearing upon this point.

> The church of the living God, the pillar and ground of the truth (1 Tim. 3:15).

The word *church* has suffered very much from the hands of men. Strangely, but frequently, has it been used to designate a mass of bricks and mortar. *Ecclesia,* "a chosen assembly," has actually by the natural debasement of the tongue of priests come down to mean a building. By no possible construction can it mean any such thing. A more debasing use of a divine word than that can scarcely be found. The word *church* has also been used by many to signify the clergy. A young man is to enter the church, that is, he is to take holy orders, to become a preacher and an authorized dispenser of the sacraments, as they are called. He is to aspire after an incumbency and is to be recognized as an ordained minister of the Word.

Now, the word *church* in Scripture means nothing like that. Such a use of terms is but confusion. It is taking God's words, mauling and destroying their sense, and then using them for our own purposes. The "church of Christ," according to the Scripture, is assembly of faithful men. *Ecclesia* originally signified assembly, not a mob, but an assembly of persons who were called together on account of their special right to meet for the discussion of certain subjects. They were a called-out assembly. The "church of God" itself, in its full sense, is a company of persons called out by the Holy Spirit from among the rest of mankind, banded together for the holy purpose of the defense and the propagation of the truth. If there be but three or four, yet if they be so banded together in the fear of God, they are to all intents and purposes a church. If they should happen to number thousands, they are no more a church on account of their numbers—a church being a company of faithful men.

To our minds, the Scripture seems very explicit as to how this church should be ordered. We believe that every church member should have equal rights and privileges; that there is no power in church officers to execute anything unless they have the full authorization of the members of the church. We believe, however, that the church should choose its pastor and, having chosen him, that they should love him and respect him for his work's sake. We also believe that with him should be associated the deacons of the church to take the oversight of pecuniary matters, and the elders of the church to assist in all the works of the pastorate in the fear of God, being overseers of the flock. Such a church we believe to be scripturally ordered. If it abide in the faith—rooted and grounded and settled—such a church may expect the benediction of heaven, and so it shall become the pillar and ground of the truth.

But what is intended in our text by saying that the church of God is the pillar and ground of the truth? When you go outside this building you may observe the use of a pillar, and that part of it that forms a basement upon which the circular stone rests exactly answers to what the apostle means by the "ground of the truth." It is the business of the church, of course, to uphold the truth in its deep foundations, to conserve and preserve it intact—thus it is the ground. To lift it up and bear it aloft in beauty and in all its fair proportions, in this the church, of course, is the pillar of the truth. Some commentators say that as pillars were used of old to bear inscriptions, as upon pillars even the brazen decrees of the Roman senate were exhibited to the people, so the church of Christ is intended to be a pillar bearing the inscription of the truth, so that it not only maintains it and upholds it, but sets it forth. At any rate, I think you will perceive in a moment that the simple meaning of my text is just this: It is the business of the church of God to maintain, to propagate, to uphold, to spread, and to defend the truth as it is in Jesus, wherever that church may be placed.

I shall use the text this morning in four ways: (1) to correct certain mistakes, (2) to convince our judgments of the excellency of God's ordinance in this matter, (3) to awaken reflections upon the subject, and (4) to suggest some ways of making this church, and every church, the pillar and ground of the truth.

Correcting Certain Mistakes

We are all deeply impressed with the importance of maintaining the doctrines of the Gospel and the truths of Christ as pure and simple as we find them in the New Testament. There are Christians who, in their extreme anxiety to accomplish this end, suggest methods that are not warranted by the text. For the rule here laid down is that the church is itself to maintain and to be the guardian of the truth. But these people, in their great anxiety to maintain it, have suggested other ways.

One of the first has been the drawing up of a *creed.* The articles of the faith shall be written out clearly and unmistakably. At a general synod every word of these articles shall be argued, any discrepancy shall be removed, and the articles shall, as nearly as possible, express the orthodox creed. It is done. The ministers assembled go home and say that creed will be the pillar and ground of the truth. As long as the name of the Westminster Assembly Confession shall be known, the truth will be safe; as long as the thirty-nine articles of the Church of England shall stand, that church must be free from error.

Ah, how signally they have failed! Especially let us take the glaring instance of the Church of England. The articles of the Church of England are Calvinistic. No person who is not deluded or dishonest can read them without seeing that the pen was dipped in Geneva ink that wrote those articles. And yet, how many Church of England clergy are as wide from anything like Calvinism as the wildest Pelagian could be supposed to be. There are, it is true, and God be glorified for it, many who do believe these articles and preach them faithfully, too. We love them and honor them for the truth's sake. But is there one in ten, no, is there one in twenty, who really receives those articles in their pure and simple meaning! If this were all, it would not be so bad. But men have had the impudence to subscribe to those articles of the church when they have not believed a single one of them and have been infidels. You have had of late, and it is not necessary for me to allude to the matter, a glaring proof that no articles whatever can conserve and maintain the truth, for men will sign them when they do not believe a word they set forth.

We have been led to think we have grown a little wiser, and we have tried to maintain the truth by our *trust deeds*. Our friends have, as they thought, put the truth in the trust deeds. It is enacted that if a minister does not preach the doctrines, the trustees shall see that he is dismissed. Ah, a very poor pillar and ground of truth this is. Our strict Baptist friends—I am not now about to enter into the question whether they are right or wrong, but supposing they are right for the moment—have been exceedingly wise in putting the strict Baptist clause into their trust deed. I am not now about to dispute the verdicts of the judges, but their clauses have been broken and their bands have been like green withes. I know a chapel now, in Norfolk, that has on the forefront over the door these words printed in stone, "For the strict Baptists forever." Really there is something fine and heroic in that, but equally ridiculous and absurd. The place will not be for the strict Baptists forever, nor will any trust deed ever be so written but that you may drive a coach and horses through, just as surely as you can through an Act of Parliament. That never was and never will be the way to maintain the truth. Let it be done if you like, but do not imagine that your trust deed is a pillar and ground of the truth.

We have fallen into a similar mistake with regard to the diffusion of the truth. In order to spread the doctrines of the Gospel, we have formed *societies*. There are missionary societies appended to every denomination. These societies are to be pillars and grounds of the truth, not so much in the maintenance of the truth as in the spreading of it. To become a member of a missionary society, you have only to subscribe to it. If you were an infidel and subscribed, you would become a member. Nothing whatsoever is required of you but that you should simply give a money qualification, and you become a member of that society. We have been wondering why our societies have not had greater success. I believe the reason is because there is not a single word in the Book of God about anything of the kind. The church of God is the pillar and ground of the truth, not a society. The church of God never ought to have delegated to any society whatsoever a work that it behooved her to have done herself. Instead of sending our subscriptions to associations, we ought to have picked our own men out of our own midst and found the means to send them forth to preach the truth as it is in Jesus ourselves. We have given up the work of the education of our young men to our colleges. I will not say they have done it ill. But I do dare to say they have not done it well. The reason, I think, has been because there is nothing in the Word of God that could warrant their accepting the trust. The church of God, not a college, is the pillar and ground of the truth. Every church should itself see to the education of its own young men. It should look out for its own evangelists. It should train its own soldiers and send them forth to the fight. The church of God will never see things done rightly if, shirking her own responsibility, she tries to cast it upon other men. Yes, if those men could be the best of men, if they were angelic, if you could find superhuman beings, yet God never called them to the work; He will not therefore honor them in it. The church, the church, the church of God—the assembly of believers—is, according to God's Word, to hold forth His truth and to be the pillar and ground of the truth.

Many have thought, however, that the truth would be quite safe in the hands of *ministers*. If we could not leave its preaching to the society, at least let the minister, so intimately connected with the church, become the pillar and ground of the truth. It is a melancholy fact that heresy never yet began with the people but with the minister. And I speak what I do know; the hearts of the people of our denomination are sounder in the truth than the hearts of the preachers. There is not a denomination under heaven that has a sincerer love to all Calvinistic doctrines than our own. Yet how many of our ministers there are who, while they do not preach against them, and I hope secretly believe them, nevertheless, are silent upon the subject. They keep it back, perhaps imagining it would not be profitable to their hearers. But there is scarcely a church in London in which there are not men and women grumbling, groaning, and murmuring because the full truth is not preached to them, and they do not hear the Word by which alone they live. There are churches in London where the truth is fully preached—blessed be God—and there you will find none who are groaning because they are famished. But there is not a church of the other sort in which there are not many disaffected persons who are thoroughly ready to come out at any moment and leave their minister if he will not give them the whole truth, instead of keeping part of it back.

You must not trust the ministry. If you rely upon us, you will rely upon broken reeds. However honest we may be, yet we have not to deal so much with the world and with its cares and troubles as you. I think your dealing with the world casts you back very often upon the old, solid realities, because in the hard daily struggle that you have to carry on you need to have the finest of the wheat to sustain your strength. Let us uplift as a great truth that the church has too much forgotten the words of the text, "The church of the living God, the pillar and ground of the truth." Not trust deeds nor yet church articles. And the church of the living God is the pillar to set forth and proclaim the truth, not the ministry, not societies, not authors, not any set of men to whom it can be delegated, but the church of God, and the church of God alone.

Now, do not misunderstand me. I would not say a single word against any society for the spread of God's truth. But I must repeat yet again that all societies of that sort spring from an irregular and unscriptural position of the church. This church, if she were in her right state, would do the whole of the work herself. The city missionary would be a member of the church, sent out and supported by the church itself. The missionary to foreign lands would have the church at his back to whom he would look for support both in prayers and in subscriptions. Every work would be performed not through this secretary or that but through the church itself. This, I believe, is the principle that will work a radical cure in all the errors that have been made and will bring back the state and system of evangelization into a proper and healthy condition. I may be wrong, but this has deeply lain upon my soul. I shall never be satisfied until I see in this church an organization so complete that it does not need a supplement, able to do every good work and fulfill every needful office of itself and by itself, welcoming ever the cooperation of others, but never needing to depend upon a society for the accomplishment of any purpose to which the Lord God has been pleased to call it.

The Excellency of God's Ordinance

Let us now note the wisdom of God in making this matter so, presuming, of course, that we have thus far rightly interpreted the will of God concerning us.

The church of God in Scripture is called a mother. What is a mother's business? What is a mother's duty? A mother's duty is to feed her own child from her own bosom. She loses a joy herself and inflicts a serious injury upon her offspring when if having the ability, she lacks the affection that would constrain her to support her own child from the fountains that God Himself has opened. And as the church of Christ is a mother, she shall lack the greatest joy and lose the sweetest privilege unless she herself trains her own children and gives them the unadulterated milk of the Word. She has no right to put her children out to nurse. How shall they love her? What affection shall they bear toward her? No, let her do as she should and keep her children at home and supply them herself. It is a mother's business, as that child grows up, to train and teach it. Let her teach it the first letters of the alphabet. Let it gather its first knowledge of Christ from a mother's lips. Who so fit to teach as she that brought it forth? None can teach so sweetly and none so effectually as she. Let her not give up the training of her child to another.

And why should we, the church of Christ, give up our children, when we first taught them to speak in Christ's name, to be trained and to be taught by others? No, by every motherly feeling that remains within the bosom of Christ's church, let her see her children brought up at her own knees, dandled there in her own lap, and not give up the work of training her sons and daughters to others. And who so fit as the mother of the family to inspire her son with holy ardor when at last he goes forward to the battle of life? Who shall give him the affectionate advice? Who shall give him the cheering word that shall sustain him in the hour of difficulty, so well as a mother whom he loves? And let the church of God, when her young men go forth to her battles, put her hand upon their shoulders and say, "Be strong, young man, be strong and dishonor not the mother that bare you, but go forth and, like the son of a Spartan mother, return not but in glory. Go forth to conquer or to die. Come back on your shield or with it, a hero or a martyr." Who can speak the words so well and sing at home so powerfully as the mother to her son or the church to her child? The church, then, has no right to delegate to another her own work. Let her bring forth her own children; let her give them nourishment; let her train them up; let her send them forth to do the Master's work.

But, then, my friends, the church is often compared to a city. Christians are the citizens. Who so fit to fight the battles of a country as the countrymen themselves? Shall we give up to a tribe of mercenaries the defense of this stalwart island? Shall we hire foreigners from afar and say to them, "Dash the invader from our own shores?" No, my friends, Britain's true hearts would wake up and Britain's strong arms would wield the weapons, if invasion should ever take place. The liberties of a country are not safe with an army but with the citizens themselves. We must be our own defenders if the land is to be preserved. There is no body of troops more fit than those who fight for their own children, their own wives, their own hearths, and the altars of their own land. Shall we, then, the church of God, seek out others besides our own citizens? Shall we give the command of our armies to those who belong not to us? Shall we send our sons and daughters out to be enrolled in other armies? No, in the name of the living God, let the church of Christ train her own citizens for the battle of Christ. Let her bring up her own young warriors for the defense and maintenance of the truth. Besides, who is there who will naturally care for this matter like the church?

My dear friends, if I were the minister of a society, I would be in a miserable plight. What would the society care for me? What would they care about what I did if there could be but a smart report sent in at the end of the year to be read at the public meeting amid the clapping of hands, and so forth? The secretary would smile upon me, but what would they care for me? What prayers would I have from the subscribers? How would I be likely to be carried on the heart of the secretary? Good man, he has twenty other agents to think of. How would he be thinking of me? But I am a minister of a church, and there is not one member of this church but that prays for me. I know that as often as you bow your knee at the family altar, you mention my name as you mention the name of your son and your daughter. Many a proof have I had from you that I am as much loved by you as if I were your brother according to the flesh. Your prayers make me strong; your sympathies make me blest. They cheer my heart and bear me up amidst the waves of calumny.

And who shall care for anything when God and the church are with him? So, then, if it be so with a minister, it must be very much more so with a missionary in the foreign land. "Why," says he, "who will pray for me? The missionary society has sent me out. The secretary knows about me. She reads my letters when I send them to her. They are put in the newsletter." But suppose some young man from these galleries was sent out to preach the Word, why we should all notice him. When the letter came from John So-and-so at Canton, and we read it at the prayer meeting, how should we pray for him! We should feel he was one of ourselves. When we made the collection for his support, we should give far more liberally than for another that we never saw, who had no connection with us and—however good the man might be—was not a personal friend of ours.

The church of God can naturally care for the state of her own ministers and her own missionaries. Ministers or missionaries cannot hope to be greatly blessed until they are under the church and not under a society. Just so with the young men for the ministry. When they go to college, they do not, I suppose, expect many people to care about them there. But with regard to those we have in our midst, why there is nothing that any of you would not cheerfully do for them. As soon as there is a new face seen among them, some of the elders of the church are sure to get him into their houses, are sure to speak kindly with him—*until I fall into another difficulty.* Sometimes my friends take the young men away too much, are too kind to them, and get the young men away from their studies in order to be with them when they ought rather to be sticking fast by their books. I find no lack of sympathy, and I know the men are happier. I believe they have greater motives to be holy because they are watched more, observed more by the members of the church. Anything that they do ill would reflect discredit upon the whole of us. When they do that which is right and honorable, there is a sort of esprit de corps that makes them long to distinguish themselves that the whole church may share in the honor of their connection. I am persuaded that this is a right principle, and I shall not cease to advocate it unless I find arguments by which it can be disproved.

And after all, my friends, who should care for the cause of Christ like the church? Oh, what reason you and I have for loving Christ's cause! Dear have been the places where we have worshiped to some of us, for there we first found the Savior. Some of you, not long ago, were the servants of sin and Satan. You were at a distance from God, and you loved that distance well. Could we not cast our eyes around and remember how some of you were drunkards and swearers and such? But you are washed, you are sanctified. Now you rejoice in Him who loved you, for He has washed you in His own blood. Now you can sing of pardoning grace and dying love. Who like you, my friends, to propagate the Gospel? Who makes such preachers as these Pauls who preach the faith that they once destroyed? Who will stand so well at the back of every agent for Christ as those who have themselves tasted and felt and handled the good Word of life? Truly the Word of God is safe in the hands of the church when the church lives near to God. When you are sensible of your gratitude to Christ, when you are conscious of your obligations to eternal and sovereign mercy, then it is that you will be pillars of the truth. You will maintain and uphold it, not shunning to declare the whole counsel of God, not hesitating to support those who endeavor to do it in your names. Thus the church is made the salt of the earth and the light of the world, irrespective of any society whatsoever. The church of God is the pillar and ground of the truth.

Reflections upon the Subject

"Well," said one, "I am afraid it would not work." That is it, my friends, that is just the hitch in the whole matter—it would not work.

"We have gotten a machinery," said a brother to me once, "we have gotten a machinery in our church that will go on just as well whatever the characters of the members may be."

"Then," I said to him, "depend upon it, yours is not that which God has ordained." For it seems to me that the most scriptural system of church government is that which requires the most prayer, the most faith, and the most piety to keep it going. The church of God was never meant to be an automaton. If it were, the wheels would all act of themselves. The church was meant to be a living thing, a living person. As the person cannot be supported if life be absent or if food be kept back or if breath be suspended, so should it be with the church. There should be certain solemn necessities without which she ceases to be a church—certain things that she must have and without which she cannot do her work.

I am glad that this difficulty is suggested at all, for it seems to me that if there were not this difficulty, it would not be God's plan.

"Well," said one, "if you believe the church is to do all this work, then the churches cannot yet be what they should!" I am glad you draw that inference, my friend, I am glad you do.

"Why," said one, "our churches could not support a missionary, some of them hardly support their minister." Just so, friend, but that is just because they are in a wrong state. There is hardly a church anywhere but what, if the Spirit of God were poured upon it, might do ten times as much for Christ as it is now doing. The fact is, there may be a few churches that are walking in the right road, but they are very few indeed. The objection that you bring ought to be an objection against the state of the church and not against the plan itself, for it is possible for the churches to maintain missionaries and minister, if they want to do it.

"Well," said one, "but a church must be very watchful to find young men for the ministry." Just so, I am glad you say that, for a church ought to be very watchful.

"But the minister must have a good deal to do," you say. Just so, and he ought to have a great deal to do. What is the use of a lazy minister! He is no good either to the world, to the church, or to himself. He is a dishonor to the noblest profession that can be bestowed upon the sons of men. Let him have plenty to do. It will keep him out of mischief, and it would do him good. Too much to do may be an evil, but too little to do is a curse. Let him have much to do.

"But," says another, "the minister ought to be a holy man, because if the young persons who associate with him learn ill manners, what then?" Just so, I am glad you said that. And so he should be a holy man. Among the Swiss, the Vaudois, and the Waldenses, every minister trains one young man. Those pastors or shepherds always have a younger brother to travel with them wherever they go. He watches the elder pastor, observes his ways, listens to his holy prayers, is inspired with his spirit, learns to tread the craggy mountains with him, learns to defy the Enemy through the course that he sees in his elder brother. He learns lessons of wisdom that are not to be learned from books, lessons of practical pastoral training that are not to be gathered from the best professors of the best colleges in the world. And thus the Swiss have ever maintained a succession of men, perhaps not brilliant, but always useful; perhaps not popular, but always sound and valiant in their defense of the truth.

And should it not be so with the church! If to carry it out it need a laborious ministry, so much the better. If it need a holy and wise ministry, much the better. No other man should be a minister at all. If it need a watchful church and a prayerful church and a church that consecrates liberally of its substance to the Lord, I say so much the better, for so ought every church to be. The only question is: Are we in the right state now to accomplish all the Lord's purposes? If we be not, let us make it a matter of prayer that we may be brought into this state, for we are never healthy unless we are prepared to do whatever God calls us to do. We must be losing in our own spiritual enjoyment if we fail to have strength to carry out all the work that the Lord imposes upon us. The Lord never gives us more to do than we can do.

We had the work of building this place, and we thought we could not do it. At last we thought we could, and we did it. If we had fifty more such places to build and the Lord laid it upon our hearts to build them, we could do it if we were in a right state. Our only lack of power is lack of grace. Give the church grace, and she does not want a new exchequer. Give her grace, she does not need then to have new ministers. Give her more grace, she will not want the world's pitiful gold to endow her and make her rich. Give her grace, and you have given her all she wants. In that one word you shall have successful ministers, you shall have laborious agencies, you shall have benevolence pouring out its floods and piety consecrating all its activities for Christ.

Ways of Making the Church the Pillar and Ground of the Truth

What can we do practically to carry out this plan? Friends, before I answer that question, let me say there are some things we must take care of or else we cannot carry it out at all. We must watch lest the church be adulterated by additions that are not an increase to her strength. We must be very careful that no thought of strife, no symptom of envy, no feeling of jealousy creep in. Until now you have been as one man—undivided and undivisible. This is actually necessary in the church for the carrying out of any of her purposes. Divided we should utterly fail.

I remember a somewhat ludicrous incident that occurred to a church in which there were great quarrelings and bickerings. The minister, the deacons, and his people were all at arm's length with daggers drawn. It was determined at last that the matter should come to a settlement, and it was by mutual consent given up to the judgment of a good Christian farmer who lived in the neighborhood. He was to hear the case and write an answer to be read at the next church meeting. Our friend, the farmer, sat down to write his letter. At the same time he had a letter from a steward or tenant asking advice about his farm and by a mistake, or rather by a blessed providence as God would have it, he put the wrong letters into the envelopes, so that the letter that was intended for the church went to the steward, and that which was intended for the steward went to the church. At the church meeting, when they were all assembled, this letter was read to the church. It ran thus: "Dear friend, mind you see to the hedges well. Keep them up as best you can and take special care of the old black bull."

Now that was a most extraordinary letter to write to a church. It had been sent by mistake, but the minister, thinking it was a bona fide piece of advice, said he could not comprehend it. Some brother got up and said it was plain enough. It meant that they must be very watchful as to whom they should receive into the church. They must keep their hedges up and see there were no gaps. "And, said he, "by 'the old black bull,' I have no doubt he means that spirit of Satan that would get in and trouble and divide us." So understanding it in that sense they made up their differences, repaired their hedges, and were careful of "the old black bull." Every church must do the same, for before we can do anything for Christ, we must first be right at home. We must have peace within our borders. We must be filled with the finest wheat, or else He will not send forth His Word and make it to run very swiftly. This, I hope, will be well seen to.

What, then, are *we* to do? If the church is to do all this, brothers and sisters, what are you and I to do? As for *me,* I must take heed to myself. I am to be the leader of this people, constantly ministering to them in the Word of life. I must take care that my dedication of myself and all I have to my Lord be so complete that I would not have an objection to their knowing what I do with all I have. I must so live that they can see right through me that I desire to serve my Master and serve Him alone. Then one and all of you must say, "What must I do?" Let each, finding his own proper niche, each seaman on board the vessel finding which rope he can best handle or what part of the tackling he best understands, take his place. Then, come rocking tempests, let the ship reel; she is safe, for she is in the hand of God and in the hands of faithful men who know how to manage her right well.

The battle is to be fought. It is to be fought by Christ's army not by hirelings. What are you and I to do? I must stand at the end of the line and wave my sword and say, "Come on, comrades!" And you, with steady step advancing, with firm, bold front maintaining every inch of the ground you take, and at last—rushing in one tremendous phalanx straightway to the thick of the fight—you must carry everything before you and win the crown for King Jesus. England expects every man to do his duty, but the church of God expects it more, and must and shall have it. By Him who shall judge the quick and the dead, by Him who bought you with His blood, I adjure you, Christian men and women, see to it that you stand each of you in your place. Do, each of you, your own appointed work. And so shall Christ's kingdom come and His will be done on earth even as it is in heaven.

I think I hear a little murmuring going around the gallery and especially stopping at some of the pews. I will not indicate the persons. They are saying, "I do not belong to the church. What am I to do?" My friends, the first thing you ought to do is to join the church. You say you love the Lord Jesus Christ. Very well, if you neglect one duty, that does not excuse you from another. You are living in a state of sin as a Christian man if you omit the duty of joining yourself with the people of God. May I ask you, when the church goes to the fight, will you tarry at home? "No," you say, "I will follow with you. I will do my work. I will go as one of the camp followers." Yes, but somehow or other, those camp followers are in a very unsatisfactory state because they are not under the discipline of the officers. Though some of them can fight well a sort of guerrilla warfare, yet we would be much stronger if we could have them in the ranks.

Friends, don't you think sometimes that the world may imagine that you mean to hold hard until you see which side will win? Had you not better cast in your lot with us while the battle rages? Besides, what does the Master say? "Whosoever therefore shall confess me before men, him will I confess also before my Father which is in heaven." And what does He say to those who do not confess? "But whosoever shall deny me before men, him will I also deny before my Father which is in heaven" (Matt. 10:32–33). You do not wish for that, surely. Enlist, then, put on your Lord's regimentals. True, you can fight His battles without them, but I think you will be more in the path of obedience and the path of safety if you put on the garments of Christ and the garments of His salvation. Come! Whosoever is on the Lord's side, let him join with the Lord's hosts. If you be not, stand back and do not dare to come. But if you are, the standard is lifted and the trumpets sounded. Come, comrades! Who is for Christ? Soldiers, who is for Lord God Omnipotent? Unfurl the standard afresh today. Jehovah-nissi, the Lord is our banner, and who will stand back? Let us enroll ourselves beneath Him and say, "O Lord, go forth with our armies and grant success, for the battle is great. Without You we shall utterly fail, but with You we shall surely get the victory."

I have preached, as you will perceive, then, to the church only. I have said nothing to the unconverted. We cannot do twenty things at a time. But I would say this word before I sit down. Remember my dear hearers, if you are not numbered with the friends of Christ, you are numbered with His enemies. Will you remember that I do not mean if you are not numbered with the visible church. I mean this: if you do not love and serve Christ. He that is not with Him is against Him; he that gathers not with Him scatters abroad. You say you take neither side. It is impossible. You must be on one side or the other. Clear the field! There is no room here except for the two armies. Whosoever is not with Christ is with Satan and shall surely be trodden down when the enemies of God are trodden like straw for the dunghill. Sinner, be aware of this, that God is against you and the hosts of God are against you. The Lord give you repentance! The Lord give you faith! Come to the Captain of Salvation and ask Him to have mercy on you! Run down the old flag! Thank God it is not nailed to the mast! Let the black flag come down and let the blood-red flag run up! Now, change masters! Spirit of God, constrain them to change masters! May they no more serve the black prince, Satan, but serve under Jesus' banner, whose service is perfect freedom and whose reward is everlasting life!

May the Lord bless each one of you for Christ's sake!

NOTES

Church Ideals: The Church Instituted

George Campbell Morgan (1863–1945) was the son of a British Baptist preacher and preached his first sermon when he was thirteen years old. He had no formal training for the ministry, but his tireless devotion to the study of the Bible helped him to become one of the leading Bible teachers of his day. Rejected by the Methodists, he was ordained into the Congregational ministry. He was associated with Dwight L. Moody in the Northfield Bible conferences and as an itinerant Bible teacher. He is best known as the pastor of the Westminster Chapel, London (1904–1917 and 1933–1945). During his second term there, he had Dr. D. Martyn Lloyd-Jones as his associate.

Morgan published more than sixty books and booklets, and his sermons are found in *The Westminster Pulpit* (London: Hodder and Stoughton, 1906–1916). This sermon was taken from volume 5.

George Campbell Morgan

7

CHURCH IDEALS: THE CHURCH INSTITUTED

The church of God (Acts 20:28 KJV).

IN THE COURSE of his charge to the elders of the Ephesian church, Paul made use of the particular phrase, "the church of God." I propose to consider four certain matters that it suggests when speaking of the church of God as revealed in the New Testament: (1) its constitution, (2) its government, (3) its discipline, and (4) its work. Our theme this morning being that of the first of these four considerations, the constitution of the church.

We are arrested in the first place by the word itself, which is by no means common in earlier books of the New Testament. The word *church* is found in the gospel of Matthew only twice, in the other gospels not at all, and for the first time in the book of the Acts of the Apostles in its fifth chapter. (In the Authorized Version, the word is found in the second chapter, where it declares that, "The Lord added to the church." But the reading of the Revised Version is "The Lord added to them." As a matter of fact, the actual statement is that "The Lord added," meaning, as I believe, that these people were added not to the church, but to the Lord.) At this point in the twentieth chapter is the final occurrence of the word in this book.

Let me remind you that our word *church* has no true connection with the word of which it is a translation, save in a secondary sense. Our word is a word full of beauty, coming to us through Old English from the Greek word that signifies the Lord. Our word, therefore, simply means "the Lord's house." It was first used of the place

---

Unless otherwise indicated, all Scripture in this sermon is quoted from the *American Standard Version* of 1901.

where Christian people assembled for worship and, presently, came to be used in a higher spiritual sense of the people who assembled for worship in such a place.

The word in which we are now interested—the true word of the passage, the word of which "church" is a translation—is a word occurring often subsequently, especially in the writings of Paul. The word *ecclesia* literally means "called out," and is used of some company of people separated from others. In this book of the Acts, it is used once of the congregation of the Hebrew people in the wilderness and once—though not there translated "church" in the sense in which the men who first heard it would be most likely to understand it—of the governing body in one of the Greek cities. On the occasion of the uproar at Ephesus there was called together the "church" at Ephesus, not the Christian church, but the church of Ephesus—that is, the assembly, the governing body, in which no slave could possibly hold office.

Such is the word itself. Suffice it to say it is one of those words that Christianity apprehended and, transfiguring, consecrated to its own purpose. As to its essential meaning, it signifies a people called out into separation. As to its uses, it suggested to the men who first heard it two ideas: (1) the Hebrew idea of the congregation—the nation itself, the theocracy, the people God-governed; and (2) the Greek idea of a company of free men elected to the business of civic government. The two ideas, therefore, most probably suggested by the word to the men who first heard it from the lips of our Lord were those of a people under the direct government of God and a people exercising in the world an authority derived from their submission to the throne of God.

Now this word is used in our New Testament about thirteen times in its catholic sense, having reference to the whole church of God, and about nine times in reference to the local assemblies of the people of God—the church in Thessalonica, the church in Corinth, the church in Ephesus, the church at Smyrna, and so on. Yet the words are used so interchangeably that it becomes evident that the New Testament writers always looked upon the local assembly as a microcosm of the catholic church, and all the things declared concerning the catholic church are true concerning the local assembly.

In approaching our study of the New Testament conception of the church, we are compelled to take time with what is perhaps a somewhat old and often debated matter, that, namely, of the distinction that it is quite necessary to draw between the kingdom of God and the church of God.

There is a distinction, and before we can understand the nature or the function of the church, it is necessary that we recognize that distinction quite clearly.

The Kingdom of God

Let me begin with that very constantly recurring phrase of our Bibles and that constantly recurring phrase of the present day, "the kingdom of God," and inquire as to what it really means.

I personally am always a little afraid lest we read into it an altogether too narrow meaning. Consequently, let us first attempt to grasp something of the breadth and spaciousness of the suggestion of the phrase itself. So far as is possible, let us free our minds from all ordinary interpretation of the meaning of the phrase and from all application of the value of the phrase. Let us consider the phrase itself in order that we may understand that to which it refers.

The kingdom of God suggests first the actual rule and reign of God. Secondly, it suggests the realm over which God rules and reigns. Finally—and it is within this final thought that we generally confine our thinking—it suggests the realization of this kingdom in the history of men and in this world in which we live. We pray "Thy kingdom come," and our Master taught us so to pray. And when we pray this, we are thinking of an actual and experimental and conscious establishment of His kingdom in the world. It is right that we should so pray, we must continue so to pray, and we must work as we pray toward the establishment of the kingdom. But there is a sense in which that kingdom has already come, in which that kingdom is already established. We come into the most true understanding of the teaching of our Bible when we remember that the phrase itself means the rule and reign of God. Included within the phrase is a theology, a science of God, a doctrine of God. It assumes the divine *transcendence,* the fact that God is seated high above all the affairs of the universe. Included in it also is the fact of the divine *immanence,* His nearness to and perpetual sustenance of every atom of the universe over which He sits enthroned. It involves also the doctrine of a personal God.

I know the difficulty of using the word *personal* in this relationship, a difficulty born of the fact that we are constantly postulating the Divine personality upon the basis of our own personalities, which I submit is a wrong process of reasoning. Personality is only perfect in God. It is never perfect in man. Man is but a shadow of the Divine, a likeness, an image, a representation; so in the matter of personality there is imperfection in man while there is perfection in God.

This phrase of *the kingdom of God* involves the doctrine of the personality of God—intelligence, emotion, volition—all the essential things of human personality, but in absolute and infinite perfection.

The phrase reminds us that of this universe, of which we know so little and can know so little, God is the Creator, the Sustainer. He arranges beforehand, as Paul said in Athens, the bounds of human habitation. He fashions, as the writer of the letter to the Hebrews declared, all the ages as they come, giving them all their tones and qualities and quantities. The whole universe is the realm over which God reigns. The kingdom of God is a fact established, from which there can be no escape on the part of angels or men or demons. All are within the grasp of His government, all are compelled to yield themselves, whether willingly or unwillingly, to the sway of His power and to the ultimate purposes of His wisdom.

These are the profoundest things, the most spacious things, suggested by a phrase that we too often use as though it only had reference to things of this earth.

And at last, the phrase does stand for the establishment in this world of the kingdom, where today we are supremely impressed by sin and sorrow and sighing. There will be established the kingdom of our God, a kingdom of love and joy and peace, of perfect human well-being in individual and social, national and international relationships. The establishment of the kingdom, or kingship, of God in the world, is the last idea suggested by the phrase itself.

Now this great thought is the fundamental truth of biblical revelation. The first chapters of the first book in the Bible suggest these things preeminently. Whatever difficulties we may have concerning what we are pleased to speak of as the authenticity or the historicity of these chapters, at least we must be perfectly agreed that they teach that all things have had their origin in the will and by the power of this one God. That, as I understand it, is the fundamental teaching of the earliest chapters of the Book of Genesis. "In the beginning God created the heavens and the earth." And in all that remains of the Old Testament, that is the perpetual chord of the dominant strain. All the music, sometimes in major and sometimes in minor cadences, is true to that underlying chord, proclaiming the throne of God and the government of God. The whole history of the Hebrew people is the history of the creation of a people recognizing that fact. By obedience to it, they come to power and influence in the world. By forgetting it, they become a people scattered over the face of the whole earth. This throne and government of God, this sovereignty of God, is the great truth that runs through all the Old Testament.

When I turn to the New Testament, I find that this is still the theme. The first word falling from the lips of the forerunner of the Christ is, "Repent, for the kingdom of heaven is at hand." The first words falling from the lips of the Christ Himself as He commenced His ministry of preaching is, "Repent ye; for the kingdom of heaven is at hand" (Matt. 3:2; 4:17). The whole of His administration—judged by His ethical standards and His spiritual interpretations, by His works as well as His words—

circles around this one word, "Seek ye first his kingdom, and his righteousness; and all these things shall be added unto you" (6:33). The supreme passion of His heart, as crystallized in the prayer that He taught His disciples and that we constantly repeat, is the same. He did not teach us to pray first for the things we need individually but for the coming of God's kingdom in this world and its establishment here.

If we watch the ministry of the Lord Jesus Christ and observe His dealing with His own nation after the flesh, we find that there came a solemn and awful moment when with quiet dignity, in the metropolis of the nation and in the temple, the center of the metropolitan life, He said this most significant thing to the rulers of the people, "The kingdom of God shall be taken away from you, and shall be given to a nation bringing forth the fruits thereof" (21:43).

Or, if we remind ourselves of the first occasion upon which He used the word *church,* let us note very carefully not all the values of His announcement, but one particular emphasis thereof. To the confessor Peter He said, "I also say unto thee, that thou art Peter, and upon this rock I will build my church; and the gates of Hades shall not prevail against it. I will give unto thee the keys of the kingdom of heaven: and whatsoever thou shalt bind on earth shall be bound in heaven: and whatsoever thou shalt loose on earth shall be loosed in heaven" (16:18–19). In other words, I will make My church the standard of moral interpretation, binding or loosing the standards of conduct among the affairs of men. The keys of the kingdom were thus committed to the men who for the moment stood as the sole representation of that church that He was about to build.

Or, if we turn to those pages in the New Testament that deal with the sacred ministry of the Spirit, the fundamental fact is still that of the kingdom of God, interpreted through the Christ as the Spirit unveils the Christ; realized within the church as the Spirit creates a race of men who will say, in answer to all opposition and all persecution and all criticism, "We must obey God rather than men" (Acts 5:29). That was Peter's answer on behalf of the apostles and the whole Christian community to the criticism and opposition and persecution of the Sadducean high priest and governing board. "How dare you," said the priest, "preach in the name of Jesus when we straitly charged you not to do so?" (see v. 28). And the answer was, "We must obey God rather than men." Or, in other words, we are in the kingdom of God, submissive to His throne, recognizing no other authority that we can allow to interfere as between us and Him. We must obey God.

As we glance on at what the New Testament says concerning the future, we find that it declares that this kingdom is to be preached and realized beyond the age of the church. Eventually in one mystic passage the apostle declares that when He, the Lord Christ, has subdued all rule and authority and power to His own sway, having reigned until even death is put beneath His feet, then He shall deliver up the kingdom to the Father, that God may be all and in all.

The Church of God

Now we come to the phrase, "the church of God," which is not of the Old Testament, which no prophet ever understood. We come to the fact that no prophecy of the Old Testament has any reference to whatsoever, hidden in the past, revealed in these times—the fact of the church. The church according to this New Testament teaching is an elect race. It is a company of people called out and unified by a common life to create an entity that Christ came for and the Spirit came to abide in, which ultimately is to be complete within itself. This entity, the full and glorious vocation of which does not begin in this age but in the ages to come, nevertheless has a most intimate relationship with that master principle of the kingdom to which we have been giving our thought. The church is a company of those in the world today in whom that kingdom principle is realized, through whom that kingdom principle is manifested, through whom that kingdom fact is to be propagated among men.

Let me again refer to words of our Lord already quoted. He said to the Hebrew people, "The kingdom of God shall be taken away from you, and shall be given to a nation bringing forth the fruits thereof." When Peter wrote his letter, he described the church, among other phrases, by this suggestive one, "a holy nation" (1 Peter 2:9). The church of God then is that holy nation in the history of the world realizing the kingdom principle, manifesting the kingdom value, proclaiming the kingdom fact, propagating the kingdom forces.

Then if that be so, let us now ask, What is the constitution of this church?

The two references made to it by our Lord I have already referred to and do not propose to deal with at any length. But I am compelled to commence with them because in them I find in germ all truth concerning this elect company, the church. He said, "Thou art Peter." I would much prefer to render with absolute literalness of translation, "Thou art rock, and upon this rock I will build my church." Do not forget to link that word of Jesus at Caesarea Philippi with the first thing He ever said to this man. When He first met him He said, "Thou art Simon the son of John: thou shalt be called [rock]" (John 1:42). At Caesarea Philippi, He said, "Thou art [rock], and upon this rock I will build my church." What rock? That master principle that, obtaining in the life of this man, had changed him from weakness to massive and perpetual strength. Not the man, not the man's humanity, not the apostle, blundering and failing, but that principle which had made him rock.

And what was the principle that had made him rock? His discovery of God in Christ and of the administration of the kingship of God in Christ—"Thou art the Christ," that is, the Messiah; "the Son," that is, One showing the essential being "of the living God" (Matt. 16:16). So that the ultimate word in the confession of Peter was the living God. He recognized in Jesus the revelation of the living God, the Son. He recognized in Him the administration of the will of the living God, the Messiah. Upon that rock, that essential rock of deity, of deity revealed, of deity administered so as to change Simon from the weak changing man that he was into the man of rock, "upon this rock I will build my church."

Or more briefly, to take the second reference to the church on the part of our Lord when speaking of the church's discipline and power in prayer, He declared, "Where two or three are gathered together in my name, there am I in the midst" (Matt. 18:20). That reveals the fact that the church consists of all those who are gathered about the living Lord and who by the administration of His Holy Spirit share His very life and nature and who are the instruments of His discipline, as He is the medium of their prevailing prayer.

The next historic reference to the church is found in the fifth chapter of the Acts. What has happened? Our Lord foretold the church, and now I find the church referred to as an existing entity. Great fear came upon the whole church when the fiery discipline that purged the fellowship of the presence of Ananias and Sapphira was manifested. Then suddenly, without introduction, the church is referred to as existing. Whence came it? The answer is to be found in the second chapter of the book. By the coming of the Spirit upon a company of waiting disciples, that company was baptized into a living unity. They became one. They were joined to the Lord and became one Spirit with the Lord, and being one Spirit with the Lord, they were also so with one another. It was a baptism into life, the dawn of a new light, the power of a new love taking possession of them. The life was the life of the Christ; the light was the light of the Christ; the love was the love of the Christ—not that they loved Him, but that He loved them, and that love took possession of them and became the impulse of all their doing and serving and suffering. Behold in the Upper Room on the day of Pentecost, after the coming of the Spirit, a company of men and women who were no longer geographically near to the Lord—for He was absent as to all human appearance and presence—and no longer one sentimentally with the Lord, but one with Him by the mystic tie of spiritual life. His life and their lives made one by the baptism of the Spirit. So the church came to be.

In view of that, the apostle wrote that which we read as lesson in the Corinthian letter, "In one Spirit were we all baptized into one body, whether Jews or Greeks, whether bond or free, and were all made to drink of one Spirit. For the body is not one member, but many" (1 Cor. 12:13–14). That is the church—the Christ Himself the Head, and all individual believing men and women, baptized by the Spirit into relationship with Him, the members. It is quite independent of nationality—Jews or Greeks—and quite independent of social position—bondslaves or free men. The great baptism of the Spirit destroys the differences and creates the unity. The great baptism of the Spirit whelms human life and brings it to the realization of its own powers by linking it to the master life, the life of the Lord and Master Himself. So was the church originally constituted. And so the church has grown through all the ages.

Paul, when in the Ephesian letter dealing with the great theme of unity (which is the theme of our morning meditation), said, "giving diligence to keep the unity of the Spirit in the bond of peace. There is one body, and one Spirit" (Eph. 4:3–4). The great vision of the catholic church filled his mind as he wrote that. Then he suddenly breaks it up, that we may see and understand it, showing us the way of entrance into this new and holy relationship: "one Lord," that is the Lord Jesus Christ presented to the vision of the individual man; "one faith," that is the faith of the man who sees the Lord, ventures everything upon Him, trusts in Him; "one baptism," that is the baptism of the Holy Spirit whereby that believing soul is made a member of that one Lord. So the church has grown through all the ages. No man has ever been made a member of the church by the vote of a church meeting or having his name written upon a society class book. All these things may be valuable in their place, but they are external and accidental. Men become members of this great church of God when the Lord is presented. They call Him Lord by faith and as a result of the Spirit's interpretation.

Then by the Spirit's baptism they are made sharers of His very life, sharers of His very nature.

And what is the purpose of this church? Let Paul finish that which I have partially quoted in the Ephesian paragraph, and we shall know. "One God and Father of all, who is over all, and through all, and in all" (v. 6). The church is the one body—the members and the Christ; the way into the church—one Lord presented, one faith exercised, one baptism received; the issue of the church—the kingdom of God, one God and Father, over all and through all and in all. The kingdom of God realized, manifested, proclaimed.

Therefore, I am a member of this catholic church, if I have believed on this one Lord and have received the baptism of the Spirit whereby I am made a member of this Lord. The baptism of the Spirit is not a second blessing; the filling may be and the endowment for power certainly is. But we cannot interpret our doctrine of the Spirit, in the light of the New Testament, without recognizing that the baptism, the whelming into life, is in answer to that faith whereby a man becomes a member of the Lord.

The first practical value of this teaching is that of a recognition on our part of the unity of the church. Friends, are we praying as we ought for that recognition? Are we living as we ought in order to the realization of it? To the passage already twice quoted, let me refer again. "I therefore, the prisoner in the Lord, beseech you to walk worthily of the calling wherewith ye were called" (v. 1 ASV). And how shall we do it? First, "giving diligence to keep the unity of the Spirit in the bond of peace." I always feel that I want to change that translation a little. Not that it is inaccurate, but that we have such strange ideas of what *keeping* may mean. "Giving diligence to keep" does not mean to guard as with a garrison. That is the thought when Paul says, "I know him whom I have believed, and I am persuaded that he is able to [keep]" (2 Tim. 1:12). The word there means to guard as with a garrison. But that is not the word here. I do no violence, no, I illuminate the passage by translating thus, "Giving diligence to keep in view the unity of the Spirit," not to create it. We cannot create unity. We can keep it in view, never forget it, and live in the power of the fact of it.

Then remember, it is the unity of the Spirit, not the unanimity of the mind. There may be many mental moods and methods of approach to the great fact of the Lord Himself and His church. Not the uniformity of the body—I care very little, less and less for that—but the unity, the oneness of the Spirit. In proportion as the church of God comes to that recognition, that keeping in view, with the corresponding answer of life to the fact of the unity of the Spirit, in that proportion we shall be content to sympathize with the differing mental convictions and bodily manifestations that the church may take. These are the great lessons of study: the unity of the church, the continuity of the church, and the certainty that the church will at last be completed and be presented to the Father for all that high and awe-inspiring vocation that lies beyond the present age.

Another practical lesson that we need to remember is that membership of the church consists in fellowship with the life of the Lord of the church. That life is light, and all the outlook is changed wherever it comes. That life is love, and the central passion and impulse of life is changed wherever it comes.

We have no right to hold any lower conception of the church than this, and no lower conception of the nature of church membership than this. If that with which I commenced be true, that the local church is, or ever should be, a microcosm of the church catholic—the realization within a limited area of all the great truth that applies to the whole fellowship—then the local church should be one consisting of all those who have seen this Lord and yielded to Him. It should be one consisting of those who have received by the Spirit's baptism the gift of His life. It should be consisting of those whose central, burning, consuming passion therefore is the kingdom of God established in the individual life, revealed to the world, proclaimed to men, and toward the ultimate victory of which all endeavor is consecrated.

May we be, so much as is possible to us, such a church. To this end, may we who form the fellowship be such men and women as, sharing His life, yield to it for the glory of His name. Amen.

The Christian Church

Phillips Brooks (1835–1893) was ordained into the Protestant Episcopal Church in 1860 while serving in Philadelphia. He became minister of Trinity Church, Boston, in 1869, and served there for twenty-two years. In 1891 he was ordained Bishop of Massachusetts. He is best known for his *Lectures on Preaching,* which he delivered at Yale in 1877. He published many volumes of sermons and lectures.

This sermon was taken from *The Light of the World,* by Phillips Brooks, published in 1910 by E. P. Dutton.

Phillips Brooks

8

THE CHRISTIAN CHURCH

Ourselves your servants for Jesus' sake (2 Corinthians 4:5).

THE CHURCH OF CHRIST has been a power in the world for many years. More and more widely it has spread, until civilization is familiar with its presence. Over the borders of civilization it has run with its missionary influence, and in lands that once were civilized it has lingered with its persistent vitality, so that today it is hard to find any country that is the home of man wherein the Christian church has not laid the cornerstones of its truth and lifted the spire of its hope.

It is possible at least to ascribe to the intrinsic vitality of the church some of those features of her history that oftentimes seem strange. That she should have excited violent hatred as well as violent love, that she should have been variously conceived, that men should have quarreled over their various conceptions of her, that she should have actually been different things at different times—all these indisputable facts are what might naturally have been looked for in a living system made of living men. They all have come. They fill the church's history with life and movement. They bring her ever new, though ever old and still the same, to each new age. They make the question, What then is the church? a question always fit to ask and answer.

I shall not try to ask or answer it today. But on this morning when we are to ask you for your offerings for the extension of the church's work and life in our own country, for domestic missions, I should like, as it has been my custom, to draw your thoughts to one or two truths about the church and its people and its ministry that are very simple but which I am not certain that we always carry in our memories.

We go back to the New Testament for the beginnings of the church, and when we once are there—quite on the other side of all the discussions and refinements that have come in through all the Christian ages—it is wonderful how simple it all is. Jesus Christ comes and preaches the Gospel of the kingdom and manifests the life of God. He stands with His shining nature upon the hill of the truth He has to preach. He is lifted up, by and by, in the fullness of His self-sacrifice upon His cross. Toward His light, soul after soul is drawn out of the darkness. Into the power of His self-sacrifice one life after another is summoned out of its discontent. It is all personal and individual at first. "As many as received him, to them gave he power to become the sons of God" (John 1:12). It is this man and that man that is summoned. The light shines through this window and finds one laborer at his work. It smiles in through the smoke of some boisterous revel and fills some generous heart with shame. It smiles upon some dreamer and turns his dream into a purpose. It is all personal and individual. "Follow me," follow Me, and Matthew leaves his tax table standing in the street. The sons of Zebedee pull hastily in over the blue water to give themselves to the Master, who has called them from the shore.

And what came next? Why, the most natural thing in all the world—that which must always come when single men believe the same truth or are driven on by the same impulse. When did a host of scholars ever sit at the same teacher's feet and not become a school? When did a host of separate soldiers go each to fight the same enemy and not be drawn into an army? When were a multitude of atoms ever filled with one magnetism and not brought into magnetic communion with each other? All the individual believers in, and followers of, Christ become one in their common loyalty and love. And so out of the crowd of disciples comes the church.

By and by a change approaches. The fountain out of which the church life visibly has sprung, the Master who has called each of these disciples audibly to Himself, is just about to vanish from their sight. He is to be still to each of them, and to each of those who shall come after them, the same that He has always been. Still, with His unseen presence, He is to give His separate summons to every soul. The unity of His believers to the end of time is still to have the secret of its existence in the personal relation between each of them and Him. To help this invisible relation to realize itself and not to be all lost in the unseen, the gracious kindness of the Master provides two symbols that from that time forward become the pledges at once of the personal believer's belonging to the Lord and of the belonging of believers to each other. The sacraments are set like gems to hold the church into its precious unity.

Such is the church. The union of believers, outwardly manifested by the sacraments, but having its essence in the personal union of each believer's soul with Christ. I see the gates of the New Testament open outward. That life, which had been taking shape within the little world that the New Testament enclosed, goes forth so quietly, so simply to meet the larger life of the world! It is Peter coming down from the housetop to go to Cornelius at Cesarea. It is Paul crossing over from Troas into Macedonia. I see the history that has come since. And all bears testimony to the naturalness of the New Testament process by the way in which it has possessed the world. This Jesus must be a true Lord of men. This power that draws His disciples to each other must be a genuine power. These sacraments must be intrinsically natural utterances of what they try to express; for, lo, everywhere the church has built itself! In every age, in every land she stands, her single life pulsating with the multitudinous life of which she is composed, the ultimate pulsation coming from the living life of her Master to which every particle of her being immediately responds. The two jewels on her breastplate are burning with ever-deepening and accumulating richness and are making together the clasp that holds about her essential nature the robe of her outward form.

This is the Christian church—the most glorious because the most natural, the most natural because the most glorious of all the associations and institutions of humankind. But as yet, you see, we have not spoken of that which sometimes seems to stand forth first in people's thinking of the church. We have not spoken of the ministry, and we are right. The church exists before the ministry. Jesus has gathered His disciples. They are united each to Him, and through Him they are all united to each other. Then, one day, out of the group of those disciples He chooses twelve whom also He calls apostles. They are disciples first, and their discipleship lies behind their apostleship until the end. Out from the body of the church rise certain men, called by the Lord to whom the church belongs, in whom all that the church means shall be peculiarly represented, who shall tell its story to the world, who shall both cultivate and manifest its life. They are to build the church and to declare the church. They are not to rule the church, certainly not to be the church.

That is what has taken place ever since. Out of the great body of Christians have stood forth the Christian leaders. Now with one sort of ordination, now with another. Now with the summons of the people, now with the irresistible impulses of their own souls. Now with the direct call of God most clear and plain. But always, if they were truly ministers of Christ, with all three consenting and confederate to give them their positions—in every age, in every land—there have stood forth the church's ministers (true successors of the first apostles). Some more and some less visibly united to those earliest ministers by their forms of faith and action, but all successors of the apostles in the nature and the spirit of the work they had to do.

And that ministry, what was it, what is it, to the church? Is it the church's master? Is it the sole and solemn channel through which divine truth and the divine will comes to the waiting hearts that could know neither but for it? Is it the stream through which alone grace flows out of the fountain of grace, which is the heart of God? That were a clear idea, a most distinct and unmistakable theory. That would set the people following wherever the ministry chose to lead. That would reduce all duty to one single duty, obedience—perfect obedience to the spiritual lord. But also that would either deny or render insignificant the very fact from which, as we saw, the church took its existence. That fact is the personal communion between each believer and the Christ. That fact must not be tampered with. No ministry of any most thoroughly ordained apostle must relieve the individual soul of its responsibility or rob the individual soul of its privilege of immediate search after the truth, immediate submission to the commandment of its Lord. What then? There is only one other place for the ministry to hold. If it is not the master it must be the servant of the church. If it is not set to rule, it must rejoice to obey. To know the church to be greater than it and not its creature, to accept it as its highest duty to help the church to realize itself and to grow into the full power of the Divine Life of which it, through the relation between Christ and the souls of its individual members, is perpetually the recipient.

Ruler or servant, which shall it be? Strange how from the first the very name by which the successors of the apostles have been called has seemed to answer the question for itself. They have been ministers, and *ministers* means "servants." Strange how the greatest of them all at the beginning took pains to claim the place in which he and his brethren should stand. "Not for that we have dominion over your faith," cried Paul, "but are helpers [partakers] of your joy" (2 Cor. 1:24). And then again in those great words that I have made my text, "We preach . . . ourselves your servants for Jesus' sake." Strange that, with words like these written in the very forefront of its shining history, the church should have so loved the other notion of the rulership of the clergy, the dominion of the priest. Strange that hierarchies, splendid with pomp or subtle with intrigue, but always hard with tyranny, should have so filled the story of the Christian ages.

And yet not strange! Nothing is strange whose illustrations occur alike in every region of human life. And where is the department of living in which servantship has not always tried to turn itself into rulership and had with long delay and difficulty to be brought back to the higher idea of servantship again. Certainly it is so in government. What is the world learning after all these years except that the governor is the servant of his people? After centuries of tyranny and subjectship—centuries in which the people seemed to exist only by the ruler's permission and to have no power of originating thought and action—everything is changed. In all of civilized Christendom there is no king who dares to claim that he is anything but the people's servant, that his power came from them, and that their will must lie behind his everywhere.

That idea of servantship has never been so absolutely lost in religion as it has in politics. But if you read the story of five centuries ago or if you see the visions, which floating before the eyes of priests have been incorporated into ecclesiastical institutions, you will become aware of how the other idea—the idea of lordship—has always been pressing for assertion. Lord-bishops and lord-presbyters, church barons and church princes, popes, prelates, potentates—they all bear witness to the presence of a theory that the church exists first in the clergy and that the laity become part of the church only by the extension of the clergy's life to them. Against that theory stands up the other: that the laity are the church and that the clergy exist separate from them only to carry out the purposes of their life, to do in special and peculiar ways what it is the duty and privilege of the whole church to do—in one great word, to be the church's servants, not its lords.

There is indeed one word in our own church's use that seems at first to give a color to the other theory. The minister of any parish is called its "rector" or its "ruler." And no doubt much of the direction of the parish's affairs is given to his hands. What is his power? I take it to be very much like that which the company of any ship entrusts to one among their number whom they make their steersman. They set him at the helm. They put the rudder in his hands. They bid him watch the compass and the stars, but it is all a delegation of their power. He has no right to sail the ship to any other than the port they wish to reach. They really steer the ship in him. He is their servant still, obeying the commandment that they gave him when they said, "Guide us and help us find our way."

But then the question comes whether with such an idea of the ministry as this, is it possible to think of it and speak of it as a divine institution—as something instituted and ordained by God Himself? Why not? It all depends on where we let ourselves get into the habit of looking for the work of God and discovering the operations of His hands. If we can see God only in movements quite outside of the natural proceedings of humanity, then we shall hardly think of any ministry as being divinely ordered, unless it comes down to us in a chariot out of the sky or else a hand be reached forth from heaven to rest upon the head of the selected priest. But if we thoroughly believe that God's activity is never more potent than when His children, full of the love and fear of Him, give Him the opportunity to work through them, then surely there can be no ordination more complete or solemn than that which draws forth from the host of worshiping and working Christians here one and there another to be in special ways that which they all are in the essence of their Christianity, to be, as Paul says, helpers of their joy.

Do you or I believe that the president of the United States is less divinely called to his high place than Henry VIII or Charles I was set upon the throne of England? And yet the president is the people's servant, and the kings were tyrants. When from the depths of any nation's life there stirs a consciousness of need that finally by a deliberate choice calls forth one man and says to him, "Be our guide," and he obeys, I know not where to find a more true utterance of God's will than that.

The very methods of the early Christian life sound crude today. We read the story of how they chose Matthias by lot to fill the place of Judas. We hear their prayer to God that He will guide the drawing of the numbered disk. We watch them as they stand around with serious exalted faces waiting the result. It is all true, inspiring, and impressive. But what is it compared with the movement of God's Spirit through a church, bidding it summon this or that earnest soul to help it and to show it of His love? A group of Christian hearts is a nobler and more sensitive medium for God to speak through than a handful of pebbles in an urn. God may speak through either; surely the voice through the sacred, the divine medium of man will be the more sacred, the more divine.

There are three possible calls to every minister: the call of God, the call of his own nature, and the call of needy men. May not one almost say that no man has a right to think himself a minister who does not hear all three vocations blending into one and marking out his path to walk in past all doubt? And these three come to perfect union in the soul of him who hears the Father call one of His children to serve the rest in those great necessities that belong to them all.

And if we ask not simply about the sacredness of the ordination but about the inspiration that goes with it, the answer is no less clear. Which will inspire a man most, which will carry him most buoyantly through a long life of labor, making the last years more eager and exhilarating than the first, the joy of ruling men or the joy of serving men? He little knows what human nature is who hesitates about his answer. You may indeed feel the identity between the two. You may see how each, realized at its fullest, becomes the other; how he who rules men most wisely serves them most humbly; and he who serves men most efficiently rules them most powerfully. But taking them in their ordinary distinction from each other, it is a nobler relation to a man to serve him than it is to rule him. Rulership stifles and hardens the nature that it deals with. Servantship opens and softens it. Rulership is unsympathetic. Servantship is full of sympathy. Rulership is monotonous and works by law. Servantship is ingenious and various and free. Rulership is self-conscious. Servantship is self-forgetful. The ruler grows tired on his throne. The servant sees his working room always alive with desire and need.

One sees the young men pressing in at the gates of life, eagerly asking what there is to do in this great, busy world, and he longs to hold out to them the privilege of the Christian ministry. I see the young men of this congregation; I have seen them for almost twenty years. I have watched some of them as they have taken their places as ministers and are doing the Gospel work. I have seen the great host of them going other ways; I see the great host of them going other ways today. They turn to honest, useful, interesting work on every side. I rejoice in all that they are doing and will do, but all the time I ask myself, "Why is it that they do not more largely seek the ministry of Christ?" I would that I could put the privilege of that ministry before them as it seems to us who have long lived in it. I wish that someone here this morning might so see it that it might win his life. I believe so fully that the Christian ministry in the next fifty years is to have a nobler opportunity of usefulness and power than it has ever had in the past that I would gladly call, if I could, with the voice of a trumpet to the brave, earnest, cultivated young men who are to live in the next fifty years to enter into it and share the privilege of that work together.

And the word with which I would summon them should be that great word *service*. "Whosoever will be chief among you, let him be your servant," Jesus said (Matt. 20:27). It was an announcement not of mortification, but of satisfaction. It was not saying, "You must disappoint your desire," but "You must fulfill it." The fulfillment of life is service. And then He stretched out His arms, and with that self-assertion which no other son of man has ever dared to make, He bade them see the illustration of what He had just told them in Himself. "Even as the Son of man came not to be ministered unto, but to minister," He said (v. 28).

The man who ministers, the man who is a minister—that is, a servant—enters into the company of Jesus. He lives with Him who gave His life for men and in so doing, lived supremely. He undertakes the sympathetic study of humanity in every part. He clothes his life with honor for human nature. He believes in man as clogged, hindered, and broken, but as capable of purification and rectification by the power of God, which he may help to bring into exercise upon it, and so he undertakes his service. Is there any theory of rulership that can compare with that for the exhilaration and elevation of a devoted man?

But the ministry does not exist for the good of the ministers but for the good of the people. So it is necessary—before we are sure that any conception of the ministry is thoroughly good and true—that we should see if that theory will help the people to the best life. What then will be the effect upon the people of being taught that their ministers are indeed their ministers, their servants? There is one effect that it might produce that would indeed be a blessing. It might make the people feel and accept their true responsibility. If they are indeed the church, charged with its interests, with its progress dependent upon them, they must be full of thought and care and study. They must know how their charge is faring. Their eyes must be here at home and at the ends of the earth at the same time. They are the church, and its disgrace or honor, its success or failure, is theirs.

There have been great times, some far back in the early history, some in the modern days, in which the whole body of the church has seemed in large degree ready to claim its privilege. The problems of religion have seemed to be all men's problems. The worship of the house of God has seemed to be all men's care. The extension of the truth, the spread of missions, has enlisted all men's anxiety and ingenuity. At those times the ministers have seemed really to be what they ought to be, not strange, foreign beings dropped down from the skies or blown into a region with which they had no affinity out of some wholly alien world. They have been part and parcel of the life from which they sprang and which always lay behind them and fed them with its strength. They were the leaders of the people only as the first curling wave, which runs up farthest on the beach, is the leader of the great world of waves that stretches out behind it—all crowding forward, all uttering its shoreward impulse in the servant-wave that bears its banner and tells of its desire.

The church—our church like all the rest—falls too far short of this idea. It is too much a clergyman's church. The people sit too much and say, "Tell us what we shall think," instead of turning their own thoughts to the most sacred things and by and by being able to say, "We think this. Help us, O servants and friends of ours, to see if it be true." The people sit too much and say, "Tell us what to do," instead of coming with their hands full of plans, saying, "This needs to be done. Do it, O servants and friends of ours, and we will supply you with all the means and help you need. It is our work."

Do you not feel, even as I speak, what a breadth and freshness and freedom and variety and vitality would come into the church's thought and working if the church itself—which is the people, not the clergy—really did think and work and, with a true sense of responsibility and a true initiative impulse, accepted the privilege of their commission?

Sometimes we hear our American system of church management abused and even ridiculed. And, no doubt, it is liable to manifest theoretical objections. It is capable of being made to seem very absurd that a congregation should ask a man to come and be their teacher but insist that they will only ask him with the understanding that he believes what they believe. But, if he comes to believe otherwise than they do, he will go away and teach them no longer. Such theoretical objections are easy to draw up in telling shape, but they amount to very little. They are of no consequence whatsoever compared with the real fact of value about our system—which is, that the people are, at least declaredly, the living and effective body of the church. The power and the responsibility reside in them. They have the real apostolical succession.

Only this certainly is true—that, with a system at whose heart is such a truth, we are bound to carry that truth out into activity with vastly more completeness than we do now. It will not do for the people to hold the power and try to give the responsibility away. Power and responsibility must go together. If the church, as it ought, counts the ministers its servants, it must assume the deeper and higher and more exigent prerogatives of mastery and think and study and believe and act with the energy and earnestness of a true church of God.

There is good reason to believe that the people in all the churches—and our church as well as all the others—show signs today that they will recognize and claim their place. There is more general thought about religious truth. There is more spontaneous activity in Christian work. Men come into the church's communion less and less from mere drift and habit, more and more with serious question about what it means. If the clergyman is less reverenced as an autocrat and less consulted as an oracle, he is more used as a willing servant and more valued as a faithful friend.

For you will freely understand how, in all that I have said this morning, the word *servant* must be completely stripped of a great deal of base association before it can be put to the high use that I have claimed for it. It must be not contradictory to, but identical with, the other word that I have just linked to it, the word *friend. Servus Servorum Dei,* "the servant of the servants of God," so the most gorgeous of ecclesiastical princes has called Himself, reverting ever to the first and truest thought of what He is. And yet *Amicus Amicorum Dei,* "friend of the friends of God," surely that too must be His name. All hardness, all reluctance, all tyranny on the one side and all obsequiency on the other side must pass away. And then in an atmosphere of mutual service—which is also an atmosphere of mutual love—the lives of minister and people must give themselves each to the other, and both to the work of Christ and of His church.

The church of the millennial days shall be nothing less, nothing else than a regenerated and complete humanity. There all shall be ministers, for all shall be servants. All shall be people, for all shall be served. In these imperfect days let us watch and wait for those days of perfectness.

Let us do all we can to help their coming. Let us count no condition final until they come. Let us live in and live for and never despair of the ever-advancing, ever-enlarging church of Christ.

The Garden of the Church

George H. Morrison (1866–1928) assisted the great Alexander Whyte in Edinburgh, pastored two churches, and then became pastor in 1902 of the distinguished Wellington Church on University Avenue in Glasgow, Scotland. His preaching drew great crowds; in fact, people had to line up an hour before the services to be sure to get seats in the large auditorium. Morrison was a master of imagination in preaching, yet his messages are solidly biblical.

From his many published volumes of sermons, I have chosen this message, found in *The Afterglow of God,* published in 1912 by Hodder and Stoughton, London.

George H. Morrison

9

THE GARDEN OF THE CHURCH

A garden inclosed is my sister, my spouse (Song of Solomon 4:12).

One of the pleasant features of our modern life is the increasing love that is betrayed toward gardens. Our garden literature is richer in these days than probably it has ever been before. There was a time, not so long ago, when the only gardening books were of a practical kind. They taught the science of gardening and the art of it and the proper arrangement of the garden ground. But now we have a library of delightful books dealing with the poetry and charm of the garden, and that is a pleasant feature of life. It may be that the appeal of the garden to this age of ours is the appeal of a secluded peace. To men who are restless and distracted there is in the garden something very restful. It may be also that there is some dim hope that the God who seems to have vanished from the creeds may yet be found somehow by the pure heart walking in the garden in the cool of the day. Do you remember how one of our poets puts that?

A garden is a lovesome thing, God wot,
Rose plot,
Fringed pool,
Ferned grot.
The veriest school
Of peace, and yet the fool
Contends that God is not.
Not God? In gardens? When the eve is cool?
Nay, but I have a sign,
'Tis very sure God walks in mine.

Now in our text from the Song of Solomon we have the church likened to a garden: "A garden inclosed is my sister, my spouse." I make no apology for taking the text mystically and applying it to the bride of Christ. I believe that we shall yet come back again to a mystical interpretation of the Song. Even already some of our finest scholars refuse to see in it just an impassioned love lilt. They recognize that there is something deeper here.

In the Garden: Order Along with a Sweet and Beautiful Variety

In some of our old English homes, like that one which is described by Charles Lamb so exquisitely, there lay, outside the garden wall, a tract of land that was called the wilderness. It was only a wilderness in this respect that it was left disordered and unkempt. It was a device, rooted in laws of contrast, to increase the pleasure that the garden gave. Men saw more vividly the garden's order and its design and the arrangement of it when just beside it was this tangled thicket land. Always, as contrasted with wild nature, this is the first mark of any garden. It is the scene of perfected arrangement; it is laid out with wisdom and with skill.

And yet along with that and in the heart of it there is a wealth that even nature lacks. Along with that and in the heart of it what an infinite variety there is! Yonder court where the slum children play—there is order in it, but there is no variety. Yonder yard in which the prisoners exercise—it is designed, yet how monotonous! But this is the very genius of a garden that everywhere you have the stamp of order, yet everywhere an infinite variety that is a joy to the beholding eye. Here is every shade of coloring. Here is every variety of shape. Here are the sturdy children of the soil, and here are those who have to cling and creep. And some lift themselves up into the sun and take the light and heat as if they owned them, and others hide themselves away as if afraid.

Now does not that union of order and variety at once suggest to you the church of Christ? Think of the order of church government—of all that the eldership has meant for Scotland. Think of the order of our public worship—not ironbound but reverent and seemly. Think of the beautiful order of the sacrament, when the bread is broken and the wine is drunk—how simple it all is, yet how expressive. The church of Christ is a designed place. It has its pattern shown it on the mount. It has its offices, its ordered polity, its hours and seasons, and its ritual.

And then within all that, as in the garden where every kind of flower is blossoming, what a variety of life and of experience! The child is there, admitted in its baptism. The man is there in the midtime of his days. The aged saint is there upon whose face the light is falling from Immanuel's Land. There is the young man in his joy of strength, there the mother praying for her children, there the merchant with his large sagacity, and the quiet dreamer of poetic dreams.

Wherever today the church of Christ is living and is the bride of Him who was the Son of Man, there is still room for all within her borders. Room for the savage from the heart of Africa and for him who is cultured to his fingertips; room for the rich from palaces of royalty and for the poorest from the city slum. Every shade of experience is there, from the crudest fervor to the ripest sanctity. Every color is there, from every country, bowing in loyalty at the feet of Christ.

In the Garden: Human Service Along with Entire Dependence upon God

Every garden is the scene of labor. It reaches its beauty only through human toil. And it is there that the perfection of the garden differs from the perfection of wild nature. One of the finest descriptions of wild nature in all literature is the description of the Trossachs in Scott's *Lady of the Lake*. With what a delicate yet splendid touch does Scott describe the scene in all its tangled wealth. And yet no human hand was busy there, planting that eglantine or sowing that warrior oak. It became beautiful without the care of man.

But in the garden there is human service as truly as in the building of a house, yet always, with that incessant toil, the sense of entire dependence upon God. You might build a temple though no dew should fall and though all the weary summer should be rainless. You might build it though the storm came sweeping down and the wild floods descended with the storm. But in a garden, service is in vain unless with service the unseen is working, giving the gentle rain in its due season and the clear shining after hours of rain. It takes night and day to make the garden flourish. It takes the ministry of warmth and dew. Were these withheld then the most earnest toil would be barren as the sowing of the sand. So in a garden, more than in most scenes, we have the constant need of human service and then the utter futility of service without the gracious ministry of heaven.

Now we all know how the church of Christ has awakened wonderfully to the thought of service. Never, I take it, since the days of Pentecost has the church been laboring as she is doing now. With an enthusiasm that is very noble and with a patience that is very Christlike, wherever there is need or want or misery the church today is going out to serve. At home in every slum of every city or abroad in every country of the world, the church is among men as one who serves. Never forget that when men decry the church. There is nothing like her service in the world. It is so freely given—it is so lowly—it is so hopeful when everything seems hopeless. But I wish to God that we always realized that here again the church is as a garden and that the finest service is but a futile thing without the attendant ministry of heaven. I tremble when men say to me, "Yours is a splendidly organized congregation." We are so apt to rest on our organization, as if in *that* there were one spark of power. Touched by the fire of the Holy Spirit, you cannot have enough organization. Untouched by that, though it works perfectly, it is the mother and the nurse of death.

In the Garden: Protection Along with Liberty

Now a garden is always a protected place—"a garden *inclosed* is my sister." A wall is built—a hedge is set around it—and wall and hedge are there just to protect it. You know the gardens in our old country houses, and how you can distinguish them at once. Through the trees, looking from the highway, nothing is visible save the high brick wall. And yet you say at once that is the garden though not a flower or fruit tree may be seen—it is the wall that tells you what it is. It is protected from the foot of cattle. It is protected from the hand of thief. It is protected from the blighting wind that would sweep down and make havoc of its wealth.

Yet that protection—what is the end and aim of it? Is it repression? No, it is not repression. Its aim is that everything that grows within should have larger liberty to be itself. When you shut up prisoners within prison walls, you do not give them liberty, you take it from them. Deliberately, for the welfare of the state, you deprive them of their freedom for a season. But when you shut up flowers in a garden, it is not to deprive them of their liberty. It is that, so protected and encompassed, they may be beautiful and may bear fruit. Destroy that wall, and in a week you may have havoc in the garden beds. Destroy that wall, and when the autumn comes you may look for fruit and look for it in vain. Here is restraint, and yet it makes for freedom. Here is protection with a view to liberty. Here in the garden is a strong defense that everything that grows may reach its best.

Well now, when you think of it, does not that again suggest the church? I question if we think enough of the protection of the church of Christ. We recognize the protection of the home. We know what it means for childhood and for youth. Without it and all the discipline it brings, what a poor affair were human life! But never forget that God who in His mercy has given us the protection of the home has given us, too, the protection of the church. It guards us in our infancy by baptism and by all the keeping that baptism implies. It guards us by its congenial fellowship and by its constant opportunities of service. It guards us by its recurring worship, nowhere more needed than in town and city where men are so apt to lose in crowded days the vision and the voice of God. You can do something to protect the church, but the church can do far more to protect you. Just as you needed the home when you were children do you need the church until the last hour you live. And the joy of that tender guardianship is this, that it checks nothing that is good and beautiful but fosters everything that has been planted there, helping it to the glory of its growth.

In the Garden: Peace Along with Growth

That a garden is a place of peace, I think we are all ready to admit. Is there any more peaceful spot than an old garden? Here though the wind is blowing there is shelter. There the sun is warmer than without. The moment you have entered the old gate there is a sweet and soothing feeling of repose. And we see the flashing of a hundred wings and hear the murmur of a thousand insects, and the roar of the world seems as a sound of dreams. If anywhere a man could forget self it would be in such a haunt of ancient peace. If anywhere a man could shut the world out it would be there within the garden wall.

Yet all the time under that robe of peace what growth there is—how silent and unceasing! There is not a flower in all the garden but is pushing toward the bearing of the fruit. Peace and growth—these two are in the garden. Peace and growth—are these not in the church? Does not God call you here to be at rest and to forget the jar and noise a little? And yet the church that can so rest the soul is not a garden in any sense for you, unless through worship and sacrament and preaching, silently and slowly you are growing. See to it, I beseech you, that you are not content with what you have attained. There is rest here, but you were better anywhere if you are only here to be lulled into sweet rest. You are here to learn. You are here to be ashamed. You are here to feel how much is still to do. God grant us in the sanctuary-garden peace, and in the sanctuary-garden growth.

NOTES

How the Church Reveals the Lord: By Witness

George Campbell Morgan (1863–1945) was the son of a British Baptist preacher and preached his first sermon when he was thirteen years old. He had no formal training for the ministry, but his tireless devotion to the study of the Bible helped him to become one of the leading Bible teachers of his day. Rejected by the Methodists, he was ordained into the Congregational ministry. He was associated with Dwight L. Moody in the Northfield Bible conferences and as an itinerant Bible teacher. He is best known as the pastor of the Westminster Chapel, London (1904–1917 and 1933–1945). During his second term there, he had Dr. D. Martyn Lloyd-Jones as his associate.

Morgan published more than sixty books and booklets, and his sermons are found in *The Westminster Pulpit* (London: Hodder and Stoughton, 1906–1916). This sermon was taken from *26 Sermons by G. Campbell Morgan,* volume 2, published by College Press, Joplin, Missouri.

George Campbell Morgan

10

HOW THE CHURCH REVEALS THE LORD: BY WITNESS

> They took knowledge of them, that they had been with Jesus (Acts 4:13).

PASSING OUT INTO THE WORLD from being with the Lord, first in the cloister and then in the assembly, His witnesses reveal Him. They do so in two ways: first, by the life, which is the expression of the experience created in worship; secondly, by boldness of speech, that authentic freedom of utterance by which the secrets of the experience are explained to the world.

In dealing with the unveiling of the Lord by the lives of His witnesses, I shall keep strictly within the realm of those elements that created His personal attractiveness in the days of His flesh. First, men saw that He lived a full life, even though He did not possess the keys that men supposed were necessary to admit men into life. Secondly, they felt that He knew. There was a note of certainty and authority in what He said—not in the tone of it, not in the dogmatic method of it, but in its inherent truth. Finally, and, perhaps supremely, they found that He cared—that He cared about them—and that His interest in them was not academic, it was not artistic merely. It was living.

These are the things that will still prove attractive to men today. In proportion as Christian men and women, knowing the secrets of worship, discover His mind and are mastered by it, they will pass out into the highways of common life revealing Him, His life, His knowledge, His sympathy. He is unveiled in the lives of His witnesses,

---

Unless otherwise indicated, all Scripture in this sermon is quoted from the *American Standard Version* of 1901.

first, in the fullness of the simplicity of their lives. He is revealed, secondly, in their quiet assurance resulting from their knowledge. Finally, He is revealed in that perpetual and unmeasured service of the Christian life, which is the expression of the sympathy resulting from the mastery of the heart by the love of God.

The Witness of the Life

We begin with the witness of the life itself. I use the phrase, "the fullness of the simple life." The Christian life is not ascetic. It goes without saying that it is not voluptuous. The Christian life is not necessarily the life of luxury. That needs no argument. But it is equally true that it is not necessarily the life of poverty. The Christian life in its fullness must be considered apart from all these accidental things. In the wonderfully self-revealing writing, the Philippian letter, we have the most classic description of real Christian life: "I have learned, in whatsoever state I am, therein to be content. I know how to be abased, and I know also how to abound: in everything and in all things have I learned the secret both to be filled and to be hungry, both to abound and to be in want" (4:11–12).

It was in that connection Paul wrote the words we quote in other connections, and quite accurately, only let us remember that it was in this connection they were first written: "I can do all things in him that strengtheneth me" (v. 13).

That is a description of real Christian life. It is a life independent of conditions and, therefore, mastering the whole of them. It is a life detached from circumstances and, therefore, while never withdrawn from circumstances, compelling them to minister to itself. It is a life that will make a man in the hour of abasement full of august dignity, and in the hour of abundance he will be characterized by a quiet humility. It is a life in which a man is always a man of power. The Christian life does not ask for luxury; it is full-orbed in poverty. The Christian life does not depend upon poverty; it can flourish in the midst of luxury. It is independent, self-contained.

Consequently, it says, I know how to be abased. I know how to behave when I am down. I do not hang my head. I can do all things through Christ who strengthens me. I know how to abound. I have no objection to abundance, but I am not going to allow abundance to drown me, to stifle me, to damn me. "A man's life consisteth not in the abundance of the things which he possesseth" (Luke 12:15) is a still profounder word. It is the word of Jesus, and it embodies all that Paul wrote.

All that is theory. Now theory only becomes dynamic when it is put in practice. Let us, then, take some very simple illustrations of what the Christian life is. We will take the illustrations of the necessary things of life. When Paul was writing one of his last letters, his first to Timothy, he said: "Godliness with contentment is great gain: for we brought nothing into the world, for neither can we carry anything out; but having food and covering we shall be therewith content" (6:6–8). That is reducing life to its simplest terms—food and covering. Not food and raiment. The revisers have changed a word very properly. "Covering" is more than clothes, it is raiment and house. If a life is short of food and covering, something is radically wrong in human arrangements. Life, being thus reduced to the terms of necessity—food, raiment, home—may now be considered from the Christian standpoint.

We begin with food. The Christian knows that food is necessary. He then reduces food to the level of the necessary, bread and water. That is the biblical account of what man really needs. It is said of the righteous man: "His bread shall be given him; his waters shall be sure" (Isa. 33:16). The Christian man says, if he has bread and water, he has need of nothing else. These things are necessary and they are sacramental and they are enough. But is that all Christianity says? Does Christianity never have more in life than bread and water? That is not the meaning of Christianity. It says, I know how to abound, as surely as I know how to be abased. It is not destroyed when it has more than bread and water. All other things are superfluities to be taken with restraint, yet with thankfulness, remembering that every creation of God is good. The Christian man does not complain because he has only bread and water. It is enough. He knows how to be abased. He is independent of anything beyond that which is necessary. The Christian man does not complain when he has more than bread and water. He then prays that he may not be destroyed by the superfluities.

There is no Christianity in observing one meatless day a week and on that particular day searching the land for delicacies that are not meat but which cost more than meat! Some Christian men know a good deal about meatless days. Forgive the personal recollection, but I go back now in memory to two years of my life in which I never touched meat because I could not afford it. There was no hardship in that. I had the most glorious time. The Christian man is independent. I have not given up meat a day a week yet. I do not do anything because fussy people ask me—unless it is necessary—not even the government! The Christian man goes through life with a high dignity. His head is never lowered, and his steps are never trembling, because he is abased. Then he walks in the grandeur of his inherent humanity. But again, his head is never lifted in haughtiness and his voice never becomes arrogant when he has abundance. Then he is bending down to see if there is anybody he can help. That is Christianity.

In the matter of covering, let us take raiment first. Has Christianity anything to say about the way we dress? The Hebrew religion had a good deal to say about dress, and everything was based upon hygienic principles. The Hebrews were forbidden to wear a garment of two kinds of stuff mingled together (see Deut. 22:11). I do not say that is a Christian law. It was necessary in the climate and under the conditions in which these people lived. The principle lying behind it is that God is interested in the way we dress. Christianity says that raiment is necessary, and that, therefore, it must be characterized by comfort and the meeting of the needs of the body. Any method of dress that distorts a human body is anti-Christian and diabolical. I need make no application of that. Color and elegance are perfectly proper and supremely Christian, but they are to be conditioned by other considerations. The Christian man is wearing hodden gray! He is not at all depressed by the fact when he goes among his friends that are in broadcloth. He knows how to be abased. The Christian man is not wearing hodden gray just now; he is wearing broadcloth. Then he is not trying to impress the other men with the fact that he is in broadcloth. He knows how to abound.

What about the home? I wonder if you will be very startled if I tell you that in a passage in the Philippians I always find a wonderful description of the things that I think ought to characterize the Christian home. I do not think Paul was thinking of the home when he wrote it. He was thinking of much wider things. But I think if I could have talked with him and said: "Paul, would you put the home in there?" he would have said: "Yes, I would put everything in there."

"Whatsoever things are true, whatsoever things are honorable, whatsoever things are just, whatsoever things are pure, whatsoever things are lovely, whatsoever things are of good report" (Phil. 4:8). Let us apply all that to furniture. Some West End drawing rooms will not stand the test of it. There are many things in them that are not true, they are grotesque. They are not honorable, if you could get to know the history what lies behind them. They are not pure in their suggestion, they are not lovely, they are not of good report. All that is suggested by that description is possible in great simplicity. I have all these elements in a cottage.

In Christian homes there should not be a gimcrack table, but a strong, true, honorable table. That is Christianity. I don't wonder some modern children are gimcrack in their mental outlook and spiritual caliber, when I look at the furniture in the homes where they have been brought up. Christianity calls for the strong, the true, the honorable, the pure. And all these things are often destroyed by ostentation. Christianity will have its picture, if only one, and it need not be an original. It can be a copy. If it is a picture of life and beauty, hang it up. If you have not a single picture in your home and you have children there, starve for a day or two and buy Harold Copping's picture of Jesus with the children of all nations about Him. Where that picture hangs the home is beautiful. Christianity is independent of the accidental, but it will make a model of heaven in a two-roomed cottage. Men and women who are thus living the simple life in all its fullness are the men and women who are revealing Jesus, for that is how He lived.

Again, the fullness of the simple life is that of *the assurance that comes of the knowledge of God*. When Paul wrote to the Colossians, he told them that he was laboring and striving for them in prayer, and for those of Laodicea in the same prayer, and for us, because he said for all those who had not seen his face in the flesh, and we are in the number of them. Among other things, he prayed that we might have full assurance and understanding, that we might know the mystery of God in Christ. Full assurance is a big thing in the Christian life. Christian men and women are those of whom it may be said that all life's activity is based upon conviction. To the Christian a question is not the inspiration of conduct. The Christian man has many doubts, but he does not live by them. He lives by faith, by that which stands opposite to doubt. Tennyson said: "We have but faith, we cannot know!" I wonder! Don't you think it might be put in another way: "We have faith, and so we know!"

Faith is certainty about unseen things, and the Christian man is the man who lives by the things about which he is certain by faith. Josh Billings once wrote something to this effect: "I would reyther know a few things than be sartin of so many things that ain't so!" Now really that is very profound. The Christian man lives by the few things he knows. "He that doubteth is condemned, . . . whatsoever is not of faith is sin" (Rom. 14:23). That is apostolic. The Christian man impresses men not by the fact that he is assertive or considers himself omniscient. He knows that there are things he does not know, and there is no knowledge so valuable to the human mind as to know that it does not know. So the foundation is laid for progress. The Christian man knows he does not know, but he does not live by the things he does not know. He knows God! He knows a few great things about God. He lives by these things. That reduces life to simplicity in many directions, but it gives life a great spaciousness.

There are a great many things I do not know about God, but I know God. I do not know what God is doing today in Europe. Some people seem to know, but I do not. I can see gleams of light every now and then and hear an undertone of music, but I have not caught the melody, to say anything of the harmony. But I know God, and I am living by that knowledge today. Full assurance of understanding does not mean omniscience or the arrogance of the man who thinks he has nothing to learn. The Christian man knows his limitation of knowledge, but he is living by two or three things of which he is perfectly sure.

The Witness of Speech

Finally, the Christian witness is one whose service is the expression of his sympathy. God-centered life is always love-mastered life. What does love-mastered life mean in a world like this? It means great joy; it means acute suffering. Those hearts today that are most mastered by the compassion of God are the hearts that are suffering most in the presence of that in the midst of which we live. That means giving! Do not allow your minds to play that foolish everyday trick of imagining that when a man says "giving," he is thinking about money. The Christian man is the man who is always ready to give himself away if he can help somebody else. His eyes are always looking, and as he looks you see shining through them a great joy and the darkling pools of unfathomable pain. As he looks, he sees the need that drives him to help somebody else.

The race of men and women, youths and maidens, boys and girls, living thus, are unveiling the Lord. Through such, men will feel His attraction, and they will want to know the secret of that life. Thus will come the opportunity for the second line of witness, which is the witness of speech.

The subject of the unveiling of the Lord in the speech of His witnesses falls into two parts: the unveiling of the Lord by public preaching, and the unveiling of the Lord by private conversation.

The unveiling of the Lord by public preaching. Concerning this, I only tarry long enough to say that this is the true place and note and nature of Christian preaching. It is the explanation to the world of the secrets of the life of the church. In the very first Christian sermon that was ever recorded, that of Peter on the Day of Pentecost, we find that he was explaining to the perplexed, amazed, critical city the secret of the life of the church that had arrested their attention and aroused their interest. The Christian preacher is to correct false impressions. Said Peter, "These are not drunken, as ye suppose" (Acts 2:15). Then he is to explain the phenomena of the Christian life and expression.

Finally, he is to declare that the door is open, that men may enter the fellowship, catch the fire, see the vision, know the life. Preaching is powerless when it has nothing to explain in the realm of life. The preaching that is only a statement of theory no one wants to hear. The preacher whose preaching is the declaration of the theory that accounts for a living experience, everybody wants to hear. That is the principle of all missionary work. The pioneer missionary in the dark and distant lands has no church the secret of whose life to explain. No! but he has himself, and the message he brings to the heathen begins to attract in proportion as the heathen see something in him that they want explained. So with the church.

Someone told me only during this past week that preaching is an unutterable failure now. Well, if it is so, it is because the preacher has not very much to explain to the world. The church in Jerusalem was aflame with God, ecstatic in their joy, jubilant in their praising. The city said: "What is the matter with these people?" If preaching in London is not arresting London, why is it failing? Because there is so little difference between people who are members of the church and those who are not. The preachers have nothing to explain. Of course, there may be another side to that. It may be that preaching has not been leading people toward this experience. The fact remains that the testimony of the witnesses in public preaching is powerful when it is the explanation of the secrets of life. If there is no challenge to the city by a living church, then preaching is of very little avail.

The unveiling of the Lord by private conversation. The Lord is to be unveiled in the speech of His witnesses not merely by public preaching but by private conversation. Here I desire to say only a few words, but I want to say them carefully. Witnessing in private conversation does not mean promiscuous buttonholing of men at inopportune times to talk to them about their souls. I think more harm than good has been done in that way. If I were arranging with a builder about building a house, and he asked me if I was saved, I would put him out. I say it without hesitation from profound conviction. But it does mean readiness to buy up opportunities when they come.

Christian life creates opportunities; Christian speech buys them up. We cannot live as Christian men and women without creating opportunities. They will come most unexpectedly. They may come in business, right in the midst of professional life. People will approach you obliquely with some question that reveals the fact that they have seen that there was something in you that arrests them. It may be done half cynically to begin with, but many an apparently cynical question is really the question of a soul in its agony. A man may approach you with a half negative: You really don't believe that? And very probably he is a man who is hoping to hear you say: I do believe it—in order that he may get a new foothold. When these opportunities come, it is the mission of the Christian soul to seize them, to be ready to buy them up.

The supreme importance of this lies in the fact that no preacher can in his preaching meet all the phases of human need. There is no way in which preachers find this out more than as they get into private contact with men. We talk to men, and men talk to us. We are startled over and over again to find that something we said was not understood as we intended it should be understood, and that we missed entirely the need of a soul, although we were struggling in the neighborhood of it with a great truth. Christian preaching cannot supersede private conversation on the things of God. Every Christian soul, living in the power of the Christ life, should be able to talk of the secrets of that life when opportunity arises. I go so far as to say, and again I say it with very strong conviction, that inability to speak to any of the truth—I do not mean to speak in public; I do not mean to address a meeting; I do not mean even to teach a Sunday school class—but inability to speak of the Lord and to speak of the secret of life must surely be the outcome of poverty in experience. Words of Jesus come back to me: "Out of the abundance of the heart the mouth speaketh" (Matt. 12:34). If there be a full personal realization of Christian life, when the opportunity comes, it will not be difficult to speak. Men tell me: I cannot possibly speak to anybody about these things! I cannot talk about these things! Well, I must respect what they say, but I stand in amazement in the presence of it, because again and again the man who says that to me can talk easily enough about other things. Things that are really the things of the heart, the things that are really the things of interest can be talked about.

A generation ago, Hugh Price Hughes said that one of the greatest tragedies that ever came to the church came when the Cross was made the symbol of her service. Not the Cross, said he, but the tongue of fire is the true symbol of the church's life and service! And surely he was right.

In conclusion, let me repeat that the relation between worship and witness is of the closest. It is those who have been with Jesus that impress the world with the fact, both in life and in speech. In the holy exercise of the cloister and of the assembly, we receive the revelations that transfigure us and that we give to the world as we pass out into its highways.

> In the secret of His presence how my soul
> delights to hide!

Oh how precious are the lessons which I learn
at Jesus' side!
And my Savior rests beside me, as we hold
communion sweet;
If I tried I could not utter what He says when
thus we meet.
And whene'er we leave the silence of that
happy meeting place,
We shall bear the shining image of the
Master in our face.

The Church—A Mother

Charles Haddon Spurgeon (1834–1892) is undoubtedly the most famous minister of the nineteenth century. Converted in 1850, he united with the Baptists and soon began to preach in various places. He became pastor of the Baptist church in Waterbeach, England, in 1851, and three years later he was called to the decaying Park Street Church, London. Within a short time the work began to prosper, a new church was built and dedicated in 1861, and Spurgeon became London's most popular preacher. In 1855, he began to publish his sermons weekly; today they make up the fifty-seven volumes of *The Metropolitan Tabernacle Pulpit*. He founded a pastor's college and several orphanages.

This sermon was taken from *The Metropolitan Tabernacle Pulpit,* volume 48.

Charles Haddon Spurgeon

11

THE CHURCH—A MOTHER

> The children which thou shalt have, after thou hast lost the other, shall say again in thine ears, The place is too strait for me: give place to me that I may dwell. Then shalt thou say in thine heart, who hath begotten me these, seeing I have lost my children, and am desolate, a captive, and removing to and fro? and who hath brought up these? Behold, I was left alone; these, where had they been? (Isaiah 49:20–21).

I NEVER LIKE to look upon the Bible as merely an old Book, a relic of the past. I like to read it and think of it as a new Book, and one applicable to the present time. And I am continually compelled to regard it as such, for I find that it relates to the things passing around me. It deals with my present sorrows, my present doubts, and my present joys. It is not merely a record of the saints in olden times, it is a Book of direction for the saints of the present generation. It not merely gave consolation to those who received the promise centuries ago, but the same promise comes home fresh and sweet to us. We look upon it as being a new and present revelation from heaven to us.

At least, there are times when the Spirit takes of the words of Scripture and makes them as fresh and new to us as though an angel had just flown from heaven and, for the first time, uttered the gracious words by whispering them in our ears. And the passage that I have read bears to me, just now, though it may not to you, all the freshness and sweetness of a passage made for the occasion. If this Book had been written yesterday, I am sure it could not contain truth more applicable to me. No, if I had to have it as Muhammad's followers had the Koran, chapter by chapter just as they required it, I could not have a Bible more adapted to my daily experience and my daily needs. For so does the Holy Spirit continually take of the things of Christ and not simply apply them to us, but, apparently, He seems to adapt them to us. Or else, He brings out to the mind's eye that old original adaptation that God had placed in them, foreknowing for what purpose they would be used in after days.

I propose to comment upon this text somewhat pointedly, and I hope that the remarks I shall make upon it may be the means of leading others to take the passage as a subject of profitable meditation. I shall begin by observing that *the church is a mother*. When I have dwelt upon that idea, I shall notice that, like other mothers, *the church has sometimes to be bereaved*. Then, in the third place, I shall observe that she has another trouble, which mothers in England do not have—God grant they never may—*she is sometimes herself a captive* and wears bonds and fetters and groans in slavery. Then I have to notice, in the fourth place, the promise of the text that *this mother, despite her bereavement, despite all her captivity, shall see her family multiplied to a most extraordinary degree,* so that she shall be overwhelmed with amazement and, lifting up her eyes, shall say, "Who hath begotten me these, seeing I have lost my children, and am desolate, a captive, and removing to and fro? and who hath brought up these? Behold, I was left alone; these, where had they been?"

The Church Is a Mother

Well now, first of all, notice that the church is a mother and always did stand in that relationship to all her members. Take each member of the church individually, each is a child; take us altogether, we make up the mother, the church. The church of Rome professes to be a mother, and what a mother she has proven to be! Let the Inquisition tell how tenderly she has nursed her babes. Let conventual torture chambers tell how her little infants have been cared for. Let the stakes that once stood on Smithfield, let the gibbets and the fires all start up, and tell the story of that tender and pitiful mother! Ah! but the church of Christ is a true mother. Even when she is not continually using the name, yet is she a tender and affectionate nursing mother to all her offspring. I shall begin here very briefly to speak about this mother.

The church is a mother because it is her privilege *to bring forth into the world the spiritual children of the Lord Jesus Christ.* The church is left in the world still that she may bring out the rest of God's elect that are still hidden in the caverns and strongholds of sin. If God had willed it, He might have brought out all His children by the mere effort of His own power without the use of any instrumentality. He might have sent His grace into each individual heart in some such miraculous manner as He did into the heart of Saul when he was going toward Damascus. But He has not chosen to do so. He, who has taken the church to be His spouse and His bride, has chosen to bring men to Himself by means. Thus it is, through God's using the church—her ministers, her children, her works, her sufferings, her prayers—through making these the means of the increase of His spiritual kingdom, she proves her right to take to herself the title of mother.

But when these little ones are born, the church's business is, next, *to feed them.* It is not enough that she has brought them to Christ. It is not sufficient that, through her agency, they have been quickened and begotten again to a lively hope by the resurrection of Jesus Christ from the dead. It is her work to feed them. She gives to them the unadulterated milk of the Word. Through her ministers, through her servants, through the different agencies that she employs, she endeavors to satisfy their longing souls with the bread of life. She gives them food convenient for them. She feeds them by her doctrine, by her ordinances. She bids them come and eat and drink at her table. It is her earnest desire and effort to supply all their spiritual wants by feeding their understandings, their affections, their hearts. Every part and power of the mind and soul the church labors to feed.

Nor is she content with feeding. It is her endeavor *to train up her children.* There are some professed churches of Christ that seem to do nothing whatever in the way of training up the young in their midst. These churches, if there be any sinners converted, scarcely ever hear of it. If children are born, there is no rejoicing over them; their names are not written in the family register—the church book. They are not asked to come forward and be recognized as children of God by being baptized. They are permitted to come up, perhaps, to the church's house, but if they should offer to join her number by profession of their faith, they would be at once told that they were not yet fit to be numbered with her right royal children. But the true nursing churches do not act thus. They look out for every babe in Christ that they can find, and then they seek to instruct these babes. When they are instructed, the church receives them into her arms and takes them to be hers to be trained up for future deeds of usefulness. She trains up some of her sons to be captains in the Lord's host. She puts the sword of the Spirit into their hands and bids them use it in fighting their Master's battles. She trains up others of her sons and daughters to teach still younger ones, and these she puts into her schools. She trains up all her children, some by one means and some by another. She says to some, "Go abroad, my children, and labor for your Lord in His far-off fields and extend His kingdom wherever you can." Thus does the church well deserve the name of mother when she brings up and fosters and nurtures the children of God.

Nor is this all the church can do. She will be always ready *to nurse her children when they become sick*. For, alas! in the church's family, there are always some sickly ones, not only sick in body but sick in spirit. And never does the church appear so truly a mother as she does to these. Over these she will be, if she is what she should be, peculiarly watchful and jealous. Though the strong shall have her attention, yet the weak shall have double. Though those who are standing up shall be helped, yet those who are cast down shall be helped still more. If there be a weak lamb, if there be a wandering sheep within the church, she opens wide her eyes, and it will be her endeavor to watch most over these. She knows her duty is like her Lord's, to bind up the broken in heart and comfort those who mourn, so she continually bids her ministers bring forth sweet things out of the storehouse. She says to her servitors, "Set on the great pot and put in the precious doctrines of the Gospel, and let all these be set asimmering that there may be food for all my children. And," says she, "take care that you bring forth the wines on the lees, well refined, the fat things full of marrow, for I have some weaklings in my family who will not be strong to labor unless they have the rich cordials of the Gospel continually given to them."

Ah! and when the church is in proper order, how she will nurse the weak! Do you remember what she did in Paul's days? For what Paul did the church did. He says, "We were gentle among you, even as a nurse cherisheth her children" (1 Thess. 2:7). So will the church do, through her ministers, her officers, and, indeed, through all her members if they act up to their duty. She will be watching for the souls of men, especially for those souls that are the saddest, the most cast down, and the most subject to temptation and to trial. She will watch over them and nurse them. And she will never be happy, let me add, until she brings all her children up to her Husband's house in heaven. She is expecting Him to come by and by. When He comes, it will be her joy to meet her Husband leading her daughters with her. And she will say, "Come forth, you daughters of Jerusalem, and see Him who is greater than King Solomon crowned 'with the crown wherewith his mother crowned him in the day of his espousals'" (Song 3:11). And, at last, when she and her Husband shall be safe in the glory kingdom in heaven, then will she say, "Here am I, and the children that You have given me and that I have nursed for You. By Your help have they been kept, by Your grace have they been preserved. It has been my loving duty, as their tender mother, to nurse, cherish, nurture, and bring them up for You."

Every time I give the right hand of fellowship to a new member, especially to those just brought in from the world, I think I hear Christ's voice speaking to me and saying,

"Take [these children], and nurse [them] for me, and I will give thee thy wages" (Ex. 2:9). I say this is said to me, but I mean it is said to the entire church. I merely speak, of course, as the representative of the body. We have, whenever members are given to us, a great charge under God to nurse them for Him and, instrumentally, to advance them in the road to heaven. But, in all this, the church is a poor mother if her God is not with her. She can do nothing in bringing forth, nothing in nurturing, nothing in training, nothing in preserving, and nothing, at last, in bringing her children home unless the Holy Spirit dwells in her and sends her strength to accomplish all.

When we speak of persons joining the church, we mean that they are added to the company of God's people. We believe that the church does not consist alone of the preachers and deacons and elders but that the church is a company of faithful men and women banded together according to God's holy rule and ordinance for the propagation of the truth as it is in Jesus. Betsy the servant-maid is as much in the church as any very reverend doctor or dean is. The church, then—by which I mean the great company and body of the faithful—is a nursing mother.

The Church Is Sometimes Bereaved

The second remark that I proposed to make upon our text is that the church is sometimes bereaved. Ah! there must be coffins in every house, there must be shrouds in every family, and so is it in the church.

The church has to lose some of her children. "After thou hast lost the other," I read here. Some of her nominal children she loses *by spiritual death,* but the reason of this is because they are not really her children at all. They are those who crept in and pretended to be hers. They looked so much like hers that she could hardly tell them. For a little while, she nursed them. But, afterward, they turned out to be the offspring of Satan, and then they went away from her. But even when they go away, she is such a loving mother that, though she feared they were not her children, yet she did not like to lose them. I heard some of her children singing the other night after one of these false offspring had been found out—

> When any turn from Zion's way,
> Alas! what numbers do,
> Methinks I hear my Saviour say,
> "Wilt thou forsake me too?"

The church does not like to lose even those who are not her children.

Then, next, she loses many of her children—I mean, they go away from her—*by death temporal.* Many of the church's children are taken up above, and, somehow, though she is glad to know they are in their Father's bosom, yet she does not like to miss them. The church regrets to see the vacant seat of her dead, and especially if it has been one of her children who has been very dutiful and has striven to serve her much. She will weep full sore for such. When she lost her son Stephen, do you recollect that a whole company of her children followed him to the grave, for it is said devout men carried him to his burial and made great lamentation over him? Though the church does not sorrow as one that has no hope—though she is glad to know that her children are well provided for and taken up to dwell in their Father's house—yet it is no small suffering to see her ministers taken away and her church officers and members removed one by one, even while in their various spheres of usefulness and while faithfully serving their Lord and Master.

Then, again, the church loses her children, sometimes, *by a trying providence.* Many churches, as well as we ourselves, are in that position; we have lost our children. We have lost many simply from the fact of their having to remove to a distance, and in this way, our congregations are necessarily scattered. Some of those who used to sit under our ministry Sunday by Sunday, who came up with our great company and kept holy day, cannot now be seen in our midst. And I, if you do not, feel this as a bereavement. I cannot bear to miss the face of a single one from the members of the church. There is a sort of sacred bond of union that binds all together. I do not like any one to go away. Except, now and then, when some grow dissatisfied, then I feel it is better for them to go somewhere else—it is certainly not worse for their minister. But those who have been loving, tender children have had to leave the church—those who have striven for her good. It is a sad thing to see them separated from us, and that has happened to this church over and over again. As often as the minister has been removed from her midst, some of her children have been lost. The church book is a very checkered book to look at. As I look back upon the record of the past, I see the membership increase rapidly. A certain minister dies, and then the church is diminished and brought low. Again another comes, and a fresh company is gathered together. As soon as he removes, away they go. Thus the church suffers bereavement. Her children are removed—not into the world, let us hope. But, alas! this does happen, even with God's own children. After losing their early love in some one church, they go on wandering here and there, scarcely caring to unite themselves in church fellowship again, living unhappily, bereaved and alone, desolate and without companions.

I think I have said enough upon this point. The church, like every other mother, has sometimes to lose her children and suffer bereavement.

The Church Has Sometimes to Be Carried Away Captive

The church has sometimes to be carried away captive. How often has this happened to the church of God in the olden times! The church has been carried into foreign countries. She has been taken from her much-loved house at Jerusalem and been compelled to sit down by the waters of Babylon and weep while she remembered her ancient habitation. Her children have hung their harps upon the willows, and when their enemies came and required of them a song, they have said, "How shall we sing the LORD's song in a strange land?" (Ps. 137:4). She has been a captive, indeed, in more modern times. Since the days of Christ, the church has been a captive in another sense, namely, that sometimes she has been cruelly persecuted. Kings have sent forth their bloody edicts against her. Then the tender nursing mother, the church, has been obliged to house her children in the dens and caves of the earth. They have worshiped in catacombs by the light of candles, or perhaps with no light whatsoever. Her dearest sons have been compelled to administer the ordinance of Christ in the vaults among the dead. When the living were too unkind, then has death found them a shelter. The earth has helped the woman and in the catacombs have her children been brought forth.

Often, too, has the church been compelled to seek a refuge in foreign countries. You know how she went far into Africa, and how, again, she sought a lodging place in the fastnesses of the Alps. There, amid the snow-clad mountains, she found some little shelter from the bloodthirsty hounds of hell. And in still more modern times, the church in this land has had to fly across the waters. There, in America, the pilgrim fathers have become the founders of mightier churches than those they had left behind. Those were the times of the church's captivity. We cannot tell in this age what griefs they were that did wring the hearts of the first passengers in the *Mayflower*. When they left England and went to America, they went forth not knowing where they went. They could not meet together for worship. It was death if they ventured to preach the Gospel. But they went where they could, among the red men, be free to worship their God. Ah, those were days of removing to and fro! Then the church wept and said, "I am desolate. I am a captive. I am driven far away from my former habitation."

The same thing has sometimes happened to the church also, not in days of persecution, but in days when deadly sickness has seized upon her limbs. It has happened when, on a sudden, her energies have been dampened, her power lessened, and she has no more brought forth children or even nursed them tenderly. Days of slumber and heaviness have come over the church, and days of heresy, too; days when her ministers were no more shining lights, but, like the flax when the light is gone out, they were an offensive stench; days when her fountains have no more gushed forth with living waters, but a black, turbid, and putrefying stream; days when, instead of the bread of heaven, her children have had to eat husks; days when, instead of the pure Word of God, it was anything but the truth—the lies of Satan and the inventions of hell.

I will say no more of the church's captivity but will just observe, in the last place, that when the church has lost her children and when she herself has been made captive and removed to and fro, she has said, "Ah, me! Ah, me! My God has forgotten me. The Lord has forsaken me. I have become a widow. I will sit in the dust. I will sorrow even to the end. I will groan even in the bitterness of my spirit. Like Rachel, I will weep for my children, and I will not be satisfied or comforted because they are not."

The Church Has Had a Marvelous Increase After All Her Captivities

Never has the church lost her children without obtaining many more. You remember, when the Jewish nation seemed to be once for all cut off from the church, when the apostle said, "Seeing ye . . . judge yourselves unworthy of everlasting life, lo, we turn to the Gentiles" (Acts 13:46). The church might have sorrowed and said, "I have lost the Jews." But she found the Gentiles. Where she lost one, she found thousands. The day of her sorrow was the day of her increase. And, do you know, whenever the church has lost a martyr, she has always, soon afterward, found her numbers increased? Gathering around the stake, idle bystanders have marked the patience of the man of God. They have seen him when his hoary beard was being singed by the flames. They have watched him as his very bones cracked in the fire. They have seen him lift to heaven his burning hands and, clapping them, cry, "God is with me in the fire!" Struck with amazement, they have asked, "What is this that makes the man rejoice in a death so terrible?" And they have gone home and have retired to pray. The next day has found them knocking at the door of the church, entreating to be admitted into the sacred number of her children. The days of her bereavement have been the days of the increase of her family. When the church has been scattered and driven to and fro, it has always been for her good—it has been like the scattering of seed.

There was once a time when there was a granary full of heavenly seed. Satan knew this was destined to cover the whole earth with a glorious harvest. He was exceedingly angry concerning it. He said, "What shall I do to destroy this seed?" So he went down into the dark pit and brought up a legion of fiends. "Now," said he, "we will burst the granary door open and will take out that grain. We will cast it on the waters. We will throw it to the winds of heaven. We will throw it all away. It shall not be kept here to make a harvest on the earth." So they broke open the door and scattered the seed. Fool that he was—God was making use of him to sow the fields. Lo! the harvest sprang up, and Satan was still more full of wrath to find that he had outwitted himself. Instead of scattering the church, he had increased it. The little handful of corn on the mountaintop, when it was planted, grew and shook like Lebanon and made the fruit of the seed rejoice and flourish like the grass of the earth. Yes, my friends, you will find, in every instance in the church's history, whenever she has been made captive or has been bereaved, it has been for her good.

Now, just at this time, we are somewhat desolate. We have lost many of our children. Our hearers are compelled to wander here and there, instead of listening to the church's voice, while we ourselves are like a captive removing to and fro from one place to another where we can meet. We have been apt to say, "This is a very sad thing and very much to our hurt." But let us say that no longer—for mark, I take this to be a personal promise. I think it is a promise to the church: "The children which thou shalt have, after thou hast lost the other, shall say again in thine ears, The place is too strait for me: give place to me that I may dwell. Then shalt thou say in thine heart, Who hath begotten me these, seeing I have lost my children, and am desolate, a captive, and removing to and fro? and who hath brought up these? Behold, I was left alone; these, where had they been?" This shall be the cry of the church.

The first thing that astonishes the church, when she opens her eyes after her captivity, is to notice *the number of her children*. She formerly counted her children by the number of their graves. She said they were all dead. But, all of a sudden, she found others coming around her and calling her mother. Again she saw her house filled. They were thronging about her, and she was astonished to see so great a number. Had there been but one or two, she would have thought they were the residue spared from the hands of the enemy, but she saw the great number and was astonished. Now, sometimes, when we think of this church, which God has so greatly enlarged that we number fifteen hundred souls, we are apt to think, "What a number!" It astonishes us. "Thou shalt see greater things than these" (John 1:50), and you shall find that our removal to another place, and our apparent captivity, shall increase the number of converts. We shall be astonished as, month by month, they come before the church and bear witness of what grace has done for them. We shall say, "Who has begotten me these? Who are these that fly as a cloud and as doves to their windows?"

It was not merely their number, it was also *their character* that astonished her, for she said, "Who has begotten me *these?* I do not know them. I have lost my children. These, where had they been? Who has brought up these?" It is their character, as well as their number, that amazes her. Often, the church find's her converts run in a certain vein; a certain class of persons is brought to know the truth. But when the church removes to and fro, there is another set brought in.

Do you remember what happened once in Exeter Hall? A young man going one Sunday morning with his skates in his hand to the Serpentine, passing Exeter Hall, saw a crowd blocking up the path. He said, "What is this? There is something special going on here." He joins the crowd, and the mass behind pushes him in. The minister preaches, and the words go home to that young man's heart. They are quick and powerful—he is brought to know the Savior and is converted. Many who are not accustomed to go to one place will go to another. Many who would not enter a place consecrated to divine worship may, nevertheless, step into another building out of idle curiosity or amusement. This has happened at the Surrey Gardens. Now, when we go to another place, another class who perhaps have never been to hear the Gospel will be induced to come in. We shall say, "Who hath begotten me these? . . . These, where had they been?"

I am not a prophet nor the son of a prophet, but, before long, this will come to pass. We shall see numbers converted to God that will astonish us. Besides that, there will be among them some remarkable sinners and some remarkable saints, and when they are added to the church, they will compel us to say, Who has begotten us these? These, where had they been? Then shall you thank God that ever you had to suffer. Then shall the church rejoice that she was bereaved and that she was removed to and fro. How do I know this? Well, I know it simply because I know, if I know anything, that this passage has been applied to my heart by the Holy Spirit. It has stuck so to me and entered so thoroughly into my heart that I have not been able to get rid of it. But I have lived upon it and have felt the sweetness of it. If this does not come true, then am I certainly deceived. But let us take care that it does come true. For, while we believe the promise, it is ours to be the means, in the hand of God, of fulfilling it.

Dear brothers and sisters, pray more than you have ever done. Wrestle with God in prayer. Plead with Him that this may come true. For though He gives the promise, He says, "I will yet for this be inquired of by the house of Israel, to do it for them" (Ezek. 36:37). I pledge you this night—I cannot get you each to say "Yes," but I pledge you, as a personal favor to your minister and as an act of kindness to our loving mother the church, as a proof of your affection to your Lord and Master—I pledge you, at the family altar and in private tonight, and on, until the next Christmas day, that we meet together to plead with God for this particular blessing. Turn to this promise in your Bibles. Read the passage at your family altars, and then plead it, "Lord, You have made us to be desolate for a time. We have lost some of our children. Now grant that the children that we shall have, after we have lost these others, may cry, 'Make room for us. The place is too strait for us to dwell in.'"

One of our brethren lately said to me, "You surely do not expect to see the tabernacle crowded down the aisles, do you?" I do, indeed; I expect to see it as crowded as this chapel has ever been. I do think we shall often be moved to say, "Who hath begotten me these?" God's arm is not shortened that He cannot save, neither is His ear heavy that He cannot hear us. We shall go on, and conquer, and never cease. The God who has been with us in the past will be with us in the future, and as it has been, so shall it be still. God shall still be glorified in the salvation of men.

NOTES

Additional Sermon Resources

Great Women of the Bible **Clarence E. Macartney**
A collection of sermons from a master pulpiteer of yesterday. Macartney's unique descriptive style brings these women of the Bible to life and provides inspirational reading for all Christians.

ISBN 0-8254-3268-5 **208 pp.** **paperback**

The Greatest Questions of the Bible and of Life **Clarence E. Macartney**
Discussing questions such as What shall I do with Jesus? What must I do to be saved? If a man dies, shall he live again? and Barabbas or Jesus? Clarence E. Macartney challenges his readers to ask questions, seek the answers from the pages of Holy Scripture, and employ this method of teaching in his or her own situation to great profit.

ISBN 0-8254-3273-1 **192 pp.** **paperback**

Greatest Texts of the Bible **Clarence E. Macartney**
This collection of sermons represents some of the author's strongest and most impassioned preaching. Except for slight modifications and updating, and the insertion of Scripture references where needed, these sermons are reissued in their original form.

ISBN 0-8254-3266-9 **208 pp.** **paperback**

The Greatest Words in the Bible and in Human Speech **Clarence E. Macartney**
A group of fifteen sermons based on fifteen words and their corresponding biblical meaning and significance. Macartney explores such words as: sin, forgiveness, now, whisperer, tomorrow, why, repent, heaven, memory, prayer, death, and experience.

ISBN 0-8254-3271-5 **192 pp.** **paperback**

He Chose Twelve **Clarence E. Macartney**
This careful study of the New Testament illuminates the personality and individuality of each of the Twelve Disciples. A carefully crafted series of Bible character sketches including chapters on all the apostles as well as Paul and John the Baptist.

ISBN 0-8254-3270-7 **176 pp.** **paperback**

Paul the Man **Clarence E. Macartney**
Macartney delves deeply into Paul's background and heritage, helping twentieth-century Christians understand what made him the pivotal figure of New Testament history. Paul's life as missionary and theologian is carefully traced in this insightful work.

ISBN 0-8254-3269-3 **208 pp.** **paperback**

Twelve Great Questions About Christ **Clarence E. Macartney**
Macartney addresses commonly asked questions about the life and person of Jesus Christ. The integrity and inspiration of the Scriptures underlies the provocative answers that Dr. Macartney provides in this thoughtful book. The broad range of subject matter will inform and inspire laymen and clergy alike.

ISBN 0-8254-3267-7 **160 pp.** **paperback**

Treasury of the World's Great Sermons **Warren W. Wiersbe**
These outstanding sermons are presented from 122 of the greatest preachers. A short biographical sketch of every preacher is also included. Complete with an index of texts and sermons.

ISBN 0-8254-4002-5 **672 double-column pp.** **paperback**

Classic Sermons on the Attributes of God **Warren W. Wiersbe**
These classic sermons lay a solid foundation for the study of God's attributes such as truth, holiness, sovereignty, omnipresence, immutability, and love. Includes messages by Henry Ward Beecher, J. D. Jones, J. H. Jowett, D. L. Moody, and John Wesley.

ISBN 0-8254-4038-6 **160 pp.** **paperback**

Classic Sermons on the Birth of Christ **Warren W. Wiersbe**
The central theme of the Bible is expanded and expounded in this collection of sermons from such great preachers as Henry P. Liddon, Walter A. Maier, G. Campbell Morgan, Arthur T. Pierson, and James S. Stewart.

ISBN 0-8254-4044-0 **160 pp.** **paperback**

Classic Sermons on Christian Service **Warren W. Wiersbe**
Dynamic principles for Christian service will be found in these classic sermons by highly acclaimed pulpit masters. Warren W. Wiersbe has carefully selected sermons which describe the essential characteristics of Christian servanthood.

ISBN 0-8254-4041-6 **160 pp.** **paperback**

Classic Sermons on the Cross of Christ **Warren W. Wiersbe**
An inspiring collection of sermons on perhaps the most significant event the world ever experienced—the death of Christ. Through masterful sermons by great pulpit masters, the reader will gain a greater understanding of the theological, devotional, and practical importance of the cross of Christ.

ISBN 0-8254-4040-8 **160 pp.** **paperback**

Classic Sermons on Faith and Doubt **Warren W. Wiersbe**
A collection of 12 carefully selected sermons, the goal of which is to stimulate the growth and maturity of the believer's faith. Among the preachers represented are A. C. Dixon, J. H. Jowett, D. Martyn Lloyd-Jones, G. Campbell Morgan, and Martin Luther.

ISBN 0-8254-4028-9 **160 pp.** **paperback**

Classic Sermons on Family and Home **Warren W. Wiersbe**
The erosion of traditional family and biblical values is accelerating at an alarming rate. Dr. Wiersbe has compiled the best of classic sermons on family life to help recapture God's enduring truth for the family today.

ISBN 0-8254-4054-8 **160 pp.** **paperback**

Classic Sermons on Hope **Warren W. Wiersbe**
Crime. Poverty. Disease. Loneliness. Social upheaval. Warren W. Wiersbe has chosen twelve classic sermons on hope that will encourage the reader to face life's struggles with a confident Christian hope. Included are sermons by G. Campbell Morgan, D. L. Moody, Charles Spurgeon, and A. W. Tozer. Excellent starter material for sermon preparation; solid spiritual content for devotional readers.

ISBN 0-8254-4045-9 **160 pp.** **paperback**

Classic Sermons on the Names of God **Warren W. Wiersbe**
Any study of the names of God in Scripture will be enhanced by the classic sermons included in this collection. They feature sermons from Charles H. Spurgeon, G. Campbell Morgan, John Ker, George Morrison, Alexander MacLaren, and George Whitefield.

ISBN 0-8254-4052-1 **160 pp.** **paperback**

Classic Sermons on Overcoming Fear **Warren W. Wiersbe**
Classic sermons by such famous preachers as Alexander Maclaren, V. Raymond Edman, Clarence Macartney, George H. Morrison, Charles H. Spurgeon, George W. Truett and others. Wiersbe has chosen sermons which offer insight as well as hope for believers faced with the uncertainty of this pilgrim journey.

ISBN 0-8254-4043-2 **160 pp.** **paperback**

Classic Sermons on Prayer **Warren W. Wiersbe**
Fourteen pulpit giants present the need for and the results of a life permeated with prayer. These sermons by such famous preachers as Dwight L. Moody, G. Campbell Morgan, Charles H. Spurgeon, Reuben A. Torrey, Alexander Whyte, and others, will help you experience the strength and power of God in prayer.

ISBN 0-8254-4029-7 **160 pp.** **paperback**

Classic Sermons on the Prodigal Son **Warren W. Wiersbe**
These sermons by highly acclaimed pulpit masters offer unique insights into perhaps the most famous of Christ's parables. These sermons will provide new understanding of the relationships between the son, father and other son. Believers will also be challenged to apply the wonderful truth of the Father's love to their own lives.

ISBN 0-8254-4039-4 **160 pp.** **paperback**

Classic Sermons on the Resurrection of Christ **Warren W. Wiersbe**
These sermons represent the best in scholarship, warmed by deep inspiration and enlivened by excitement about what the Resurrection of Christ means to the believer.

ISBN 0-8254-4042-4 **160 pp.** **paperback**

Classic Sermons on the Second Coming and Other Prophetic Themes **Warren W. Wiersbe**
The second coming of Christ is a promise presented in many New Testament passages. Dr. Wiersbe has marshaled an array of classic sermons on Christ's coming by great preachers such as C. H. Spurgeon, G. Campbell Morgan, C. E. Macartney, and Alexander MacLaren.

ISBN 0-8254-4051-3 **160 pp.** **paperback**

Classic Sermons on the Sovereignty of God **Warren W. Wiersbe**
Sovereignty. All authority, power, dominion, and majesty belong to God. Warren W. Wiersbe has chosen twelve classic sermons that capture the glory and grace of this divine attribute. Included are sermons by Paul Little, R. A. Torrey, C. H. Spurgeon, and Jonathon Edwards.

0-8254-4055-6 **160 pp.** **paperback**

Classic Sermons on Spiritual Warfare **Warren W. Wiersbe**
In a timely new compilation of classic sermons, Dr. Warren Wiersbe offers eleven expositions dealing with various facets of Satanic activity. Included are sermons by such outstanding preachers as William Culbertson, Allan Redpath, D. Martyn Lloyd-Jones, G. Campbell Morgan, and C. H. Spurgeon.

ISBN 0-8254-4049-1 **160 pp.** **paperback**